OFFENSE AND DEFENSE

July 2019

United States Government
US Army

Contents

		Page
	PREFACE	iii
	INTRODUCTION	v
Chapter 1	**TACTICAL FUNDAMENTALS**	**1-1**
	Tactics	1-1
	The Tactical Level of Warfare	1-1
	The Art and Science of Tactics	1-2
	Solving Tactical Problems	1-4
	Hasty Versus Deliberate Operations	1-5
	Risk	1-6
Chapter 2	**COMMON TACTICAL CONCEPTS AND ECHELONS**	**2-1**
	Joint Interdependence	2-1
	Principles of Joint Operations	2-1
	Operational Variables	2-1
	Mission Variables	2-2
	The Army's Tactical Doctrinal Taxonomy	2-2
	Warfighting Functions	2-2
	Defeat Mechanisms	2-4
	Basic Tactical Concepts	2-4
	Forms of Maneuver and Forms of the Defense	2-17
	Echelons	2-17
Chapter 3	**THE OFFENSE**	**3-1**
	Purposes of the Offense	3-1
	Characteristics of the Offense	3-1
	Types of Offensive Operations	3-3
	Common Offensive Control Measures	3-3
	Common Offensive Planning Considerations	3-7
	Transition	3-18
Chapter 4	**THE DEFENSE**	**4-1**
	Purposes of the Defense	4-1
	Characteristics of the Defense	4-1
	Types of Defensive Operations	4-3
	Common Defensive Control Measures	4-4
	Common Defensive Planning Considerations	4-7
	Transition	4-18

DISTRIBUTION RESTRICTION: Approved for public release; distribution is unlimited.

*This publication supersedes ADP 3-90, dated 13 August 2018.

Contents

Chapter 5	ENABLING OPERATIONS	5-1
	Reconnaissance	5-1
	Security Operations	5-2
	Troop Movement	5-3
	Relief in Place	5-4
	Passage of Lines	5-4
	GLOSSARY	Glossary-1
	REFERENCES	References-1
	INDEX	Index-1

Figures

Figure 1-1. Risk reduction factors 1-7
Figure 2-1. Taxonomy of Army tactics 2-3
Figure 2-2. Division-assigned airspace 2-9
Figure 2-3. Flanks of a stationary unit 2-12
Figure 2-4. Flanks of a moving unit 2-13
Figure 4-1. Defensive arrangement 4-6

Tables

Introductory table. New and modified Army terms vi

Preface

ADP 3-90 augments the land operations doctrine established in ADP 3-0 and FM 3-0. It provides additional information on the basic concepts and control measures associated with the art and science of tactics. ADP 3-90 provides the doctrine for the conduct of offensive and defensive operations, just as ADP 3-07 provides doctrine for the conduct of stability operations, and ADP 3-28 provides the doctrine for the defense support of civil authorities tasks.

ADP 3-90 focuses on the organization of forces; minimum-essential control measures; and general planning, preparation, and execution considerations for offensive and defensive operations. It is the common reference for all students of the art and science of tactics. Echelon-specific Army techniques publications address how each tactical echelon employs these tactical concepts.

The principal audience for ADP 3-90 is all members of the profession of arms. Commanders and staffs of Army headquarters serving as a joint task force or multinational headquarters should also refer to applicable joint or multinational doctrine concerning the range of military operations. Trainers and educators throughout the Army use this publication.

Commanders, staffs, and subordinates ensure their decisions and actions comply with applicable U.S., international, and, in some cases, host-nation laws and regulations. Commanders at all levels ensure their Soldiers and Department of the Army Civilians operate in accordance with the law of war and the rules of engagement. (See FM 27-10.)

ADP 3-90 uses joint terms where applicable. Selected joint and Army terms and definitions appear in both the glossary and the text. Terms for which ADP 3-90 is the proponent publication (the authority) are marked with an asterisk (*) in the glossary. When first defined in the text, terms for which ADP 3-90 is the proponent publication are boldfaced and italicized, and definitions are boldfaced. When first defining other proponent definitions in the text, the term is italicized and the number of the proponent publication follows the definition. Following uses of the term are not italicized.

ADP 3-90 applies to the Active Army, Army National Guard/Army National Guard of the United States, and United States Army Reserve unless otherwise stated.

The proponent of ADP 3-90 is the United States Army Combined Arms Center. The preparing agency is the Combined Arms Doctrine Directorate, U.S. Army Combined Arms Center. Send comments and recommendations on a DA Form 2028 (*Recommended Changes to Publications and Blank Forms*) to Commander, U.S. Army Combined Arms Center and Fort Leavenworth, ATTN: ATZL-MCD (ADP 3-90), 300 McPherson Avenue, Fort Leavenworth, KS 66027-2337; by email to usarmy.leavenworth.mccoe.mbx.cadd-org-mailbox@mail.mil; or submit an electronic DA Form 2028.

This page intentionally left blank.

Introduction

ADP 3-90, *Offense and Defense*, articulates how Army forces conduct the offense and defense. It contains the fundamental tactics related to the execution of these elements of decisive action. Tactics employs, orders arrangement of, and directs actions of forces in relation to each other. Commanders select tactics that place their forces in positions of relative advantage. The selected tactics support the attainment of goals. Tactics create multiple dilemmas for an enemy allowing the friendly commander to defeat the enemy in detail. Successful tactics require synchronizing all the elements of combat power.

ADP 3-90 is the introductory reference for all Army professionals studying the art and science of tactics. The five chapters of ADP 3-90 focus on the tactics used to employ available means to prevail during large-scale ground combat (in the offense and the defense), and they constitute the Army's collective view of how it conducts prompt and sustained tactical offensive and defensive operations on land. All tactics require judgment in application. This publication is not prescriptive, but it is authoritative. ADP 3-90 standardizes the lexicon commanders' use to describe the conduct of offensive, defensive, and supporting enabling operations. It focuses on the employment of combined arms in combat operations.

ADP 3-90 has five chapters.

Chapter 1 introduces the art and science of tactics. The key points contained within chapter 1 include—
- An opponent is always thinking and seeking ways to prevail. Some of those ways may be considered out-of-bounds by the U.S. and unified action partner forces.
- A force is always in some form of contact.
- Mastering the art and science of tactics requires constant study and training.
- Doctrine provides a set of tools that leaders adapt to meet the needs and conditions associated with their specific situations.

Chapter 2 defines basic tactical concepts and echelons associated with the conduct of both the offense and defense. It illustrates the doctrinal taxonomy established in ADP 3-0. That doctrinal taxonomy is the basis for the organization of chapters 3 through 5. Chapter 2 also defines echelons from the fire team to the field army.

Chapter 3 provides the basics of the offense. It discusses the purposes and characteristics of the offense. It defines the four types of offensive operations. It addresses common offensive control measures and discusses common offensive planning considerations by warfighting function. The chapter closes with a discussion of transitions to either defensive or stability operations.

Chapter 4 provides the basics of the defense. It discusses the purposes and characteristics of the defense. It defines the three types of defensive operations. It addresses common defensive control measures and then discusses common defensive planning considerations by warfighting function. The chapter closes with a discussion of transitions to offensive or stability operations.

Chapter 5 addresses those enabling operations that are not the subject of their own publications. Commanders conduct enabling operations as shaping or supporting efforts during decisive action, but they are not primarily offensive, defensive, and stability operations, or defense support of civil authorities tasks. Chapter 5 introduces reconnaissance, security operations, troop movement, relief in place, and passage of lines.

ADP 3-90 is the proponent for many terms. Some terms have changed since the last version of ADP 3-90. The introductory table highlights new terms or modified definitions in this edition.

Introductory table. New and modified Army terms

Term	Remarks
administrative movement	ADP 3-90 becomes proponent.
area defense	Modifies definition.
area reconnaissance	Modifies definition.
area security	Modifies definition.
art of tactics	Modifies definition.
attack	Modifies definition.
avenue of approach	Modifies definition.
battle drill	Adds new definition.
battle handover line	Modifies definition.
breakout	Modifies definition.
bypass criteria	Modifies definition.
combat formation	No longer uses as a defined Army term.
corps	Adds new definition.
cover	Modifies definition.
delay	Adds new definition.
delaying operations	No longer uses as a defined Army term.
division	Modifies definition.
engagement area	ADP 3-90 becomes proponent and modifies definition.
exploitation	Modifies definition.
field army	Adds new definition.
guard	Modifies definition.
limit of advance	Modifies definition.
line of contact	ADP 3-90 becomes proponent.
local security	Modifies definition.
maneuver	Adds new Army definition.
meeting engagement	ADP 3-90 becomes proponent.
mobile defense	Modifies definition.
movement	Adds new definition.
movement formation	Adds new definition.
movement to contact	Modifies definition.
objective	Modifies Army definition.
objective rally point	Modifies definition.
pursuit	Modifies definition.
reconnaissance in force	Modifies definition.
reserve	Modifies Army definition.
retirement	Modifies definition.
retrograde	Modifies Army definition.
route reconnaissance	Modifies definition.
screen	Modifies definition.

Introductory table. New and modified Army terms (*continued*)

Term	Remarks
security tasks	No longer uses as a defined Army term.
security operations	Adds new definition.
sequential relief in place	Adds new definition.
simultaneous relief in place	Adds new definition.
staggered relief in place	Adds new definition.
tactics	Adds new Army definition.
troop movement	Modifies definition.
withdraw	Adds new definition.
zone reconnaissance	Modifies definition.

This page intentionally left blank.

Chapter 1
Tactical Fundamentals

Commanders consider their actions strategic, operational, or tactical based on whether they achieve a strategic, operational, or tactical objective. This chapter addresses the tactical level of warfare, the art and science of tactics, solving tactical problems, and hasty versus deliberate operations.

TACTICS

1-1. **Tactics is the employment, ordered arrangement, and directed actions of forces in relation to each other.** ADP 3-90 is the primary publication for the offense and defense at the tactical level. It is authoritative and provides guidance in the form of combat-tested concepts and ideas modified to take advantage of Army and joint capabilities. It focuses on the tactics used to employ current capabilities to prevail in combat. Tactics are not prescriptive. Tacticians use creativity to develop solutions for which enemy forces are neither prepared nor able to cope.

1-2. Tactics always require judgment and adaptation to a situation's unique circumstances. Techniques and procedures are established patterns or processes that can be applied repeatedly with little judgment to various circumstances. Together, tactics, techniques, and procedures (TTP) provide commanders and staffs with the fundamentals to develop solutions to tactical problems. The solution to any specific problem is a unique combination of these fundamentals, current TTP, and the creation of new TTP based on an evaluation of the situation. Commanders determine acceptable solutions by mastering doctrine and current TTP. They gain this mastery through experiences in education, training, and operations.

THE TACTICAL LEVEL OF WARFARE

1-3. The *tactical level of warfare* is the level of warfare at which battles and engagements are planned and executed to achieve military objectives assigned to tactical units or task forces (JP 3-0). Activities at this level focus on achieving assigned objectives through the ordered arrangement, movement, and maneuver of combat elements in relation to each other and to enemy forces. The strategic and operational levels of warfare provide the context for tactical operations. (See JP 3-0 and ADP 3-0 for more discussions on strategic and operational levels of warfare.) Without this context, tactical operations become disconnected from operational end states and strategic goals.

1-4. An *engagement* is a tactical conflict, usually between opposing lower echelon maneuver forces (JP 3-0). Brigades and lower echelon units generally conduct engagements. Engagements result from deliberate closure with or chance encounters between two opponents.

1-5. **A *battle* is a set of related engagements that lasts longer and involves larger forces than an engagement.** Battles affect the course of a campaign or major operation, as they determine the outcome of a division or corps echelon achieving one or more significant objectives. The outcomes of battles determine strategic and operational success and contribute to the overall operation or campaign achieving a strategic purpose. The outcomes of engagements determine tactical success and contribute to friendly forces winning a battle.

1-6. Echelons of command, sizes of units, types of equipment, or components do not define the strategic, operational, or tactical levels of warfare. Instead, the level of warfare is determined by what level objective is achieved by the action. National assets, including space-based and cyberspace capabilities previously considered principally strategic, provide important support to tactical operations.

Chapter 1

1-7. The levels of warfare help commanders to visualize a logical nesting of operations, to allocate resources, and to assign tasks to the appropriate echelon of command. Advances in technology and a complex information environment compress time and space relationships. This reality blurs the boundaries among the levels of warfare. In a world of constant and immediate communication, a single event may affect all three levels of warfare simultaneously.

THE ART AND SCIENCE OF TACTICS

1-8. Army leaders at all echelons master the art and science of tactics—two distinct yet inseparable concepts—to solve the problems they will face on the battlefield. A tactical problem occurs when the mission variables—mission, enemy, terrain and weather, troops and support available, time available, and civil considerations (known as METT-TC)—of the desired tactical situation differ from the current situation. (See ADP 6-0 for a discussion of the mission variables.)

THE ART OF TACTICS

1-9. **The *art of tactics* is three interrelated aspects: the creative and flexible array of means to accomplish missions, decision making under conditions of uncertainty when faced with a thinking and adaptive enemy, and the understanding of the effects of combat on Soldiers**. An art, as opposed to a science, requires exercising intuition based on operational experiences and cannot be learned solely by study. Leaders exercise the art of tactics by balancing study with a variety of relevant and practical experiences. Repetitive practice under a variety of realistic conditions increases an individual's mastery of the art of tactics.

1-10. Leaders apply the art of tactics to solve tactical problems within their commander's intent by choosing from interrelated options, including—
- The types of operations, forms of maneuver, and tactical mission tasks.
- Task organization of available forces and allocation of resources.
- The arrangement and choice of control measures.
- Controlling the tempo of the operation.
- The level of necessary risk.

1-11. Combat is a lethal clash of opposing wills and a violent struggle between thinking and adaptive commanders with opposing goals. Commanders strive to defeat their enemies. *Defeat* is to render a force incapable of achieving its objectives (ADP 3-0). Commanders seek to accomplish missions that support operational or strategic purposes while preventing their enemies from doing the same.

1-12. These options that support operational or strategic purposes represent a starting point for developing a course of action (COA) to a specific tactical problem. Each decision represents a choice among a range of options. Each option balances competing demands and requires judgment. Tacticians use experience and creativity to outthink their opposing enemy commanders. The mission variables have many combinations that make each new tactical situation unique. Because enemy forces change and adapt to friendly moves during operations, there is no guarantee that the current plan remains valid throughout a single operation.

Creative and Flexible Application of Means

1-13. The first aspect of the art of tactics is the innovative application of the means available to seize, retain, and exploit the initiative against enemy forces. These means include friendly capabilities, organizations, and materiel. Effective employment of available means requires an understanding of how friendly forces fight the offense and defense. Effective employment also requires understanding the enemy's objectives and methods it uses to organize and operate its forces.

1-14. Military forces that seize, retain, and exploit the initiative and employ movement and maneuver operate in more than just the land domain. Tactical through strategic land operations depend on the ability of Army forces to affect the behavior and capabilities of enemies, adversaries, and the local population in their area of operations (AO). The ability to influence relevant actors requires an understanding of the information environment and the ways that information affects them and military operations. Affecting their behavior and capabilities requires friendly forces effectively integrating information operations, cyberspace operations, and electronic warfare capabilities, as appropriate, to the lowest possible echelons.

Decision Making Under Conditions of Uncertainty

1-15. The second aspect of the art of tactics is decision making under conditions of uncertainty in a time-constrained environment. Leaders need a high degree of creativity and clarity of thought to understand the implications and opportunities afforded in chaotic and ambiguous situations. In this environment, the Army requires leaders who act decisively (based on their experiences), accurate running estimates, and leaders with good judgment. While detailed planning provides a level of awareness before a battle, leaders who develop situational understanding through action are the ones most likely to seize the initiative and exploit fleeting positions of relative advantage. *Situational understanding* is the product of applying analysis and judgment to relevant information to determine the relationships among the operational and mission variables (ADP 6-0).

1-16. Decision making in an uncertain environment demands leader involvement. Commanders and staffs need to master the fundamentals of the military decision-making process before they can abbreviate the process. When time does not allow for developing multiple COAs, commanders apply staff input and their experiences to direct a suitable solution. Units use warning orders to maximize parallel planning and share information with subordinates as early as possible. The use of liaison officers and collaborative systems accelerate the process.

Understanding of the Effects of Combat on Soldiers

1-17. The third and final aspect of the art of tactics is the understanding of the effects of combat on Soldiers. This understanding is what differentiates actual combat from the circumstances encountered during training. Friction resulting from violence, death, and chance characterize combat. Continuous combat operations—the conduct of the offense and defense—take a toll on Soldiers, severely straining their physical and mental stamina. The emotional responses resulting from combat influence human behavior. Loss of stamina degrades courage, confidence, and discipline. If left unchecked, these effects can result in decreased vigilance, slowed perception, inability to concentrate, poor decision making, and an inability to perform routine tasks.

1-18. Success in combat depends on understanding the emotional and physical aspects of combat as well as understanding the aspects of numerical and technological superiority. Tacticians account for these aspects of combat. They seek to cause and exploit fear and physical weakness to erode and ultimately defeat enemy forces.

1-19. Leaders must be alert to indicators of fatigue, fear, lapses in discipline or ethical standards, and reduced morale among both friendly and enemy forces. Effective leaders counter these effects on friendly forces while exploiting the effects on enemy forces. Maintaining tactical pressure causes enemy forces to react continuously and affords them no chance to recover. Pressure provides friendly forces opportunities to exploit while enemy forces become increasingly unable to mount effective resistance, which can lead to their collapse. Leaders factor the negative effects of combat on human endurance into their plans, and they understand the subtle difference between pushing Soldiers to their limits to exploit success and risking the collapse of unit cohesion.

1-20. Artful tactics require commanders to accept risk when formulating and executing plans. Success during operations depends on a willingness to embrace risk as opportunity rather than treating it as something to avoid. The best COA may be the one with the greatest risk. Successful commanders balance the tension between protecting their force and accepting risks to accomplish their mission.

THE SCIENCE OF TACTICS

1-21. **The *science of tactics* is the understanding of those military aspects of tactics—capabilities, techniques, and procedures—that can be measured and codified**. The science of tactics includes the physical capabilities of friendly and enemy organizations and systems. It also includes techniques and procedures used to accomplish specific tasks. The science of tactics is straightforward. Much of what subordinate doctrine publications contain are the science of tactics—techniques and procedures for

Chapter 1

employing the various elements of the combined arms team. A combined arms team is a team that uses *combined arms*—the synchronized and simultaneous application of arms to achieve an effect greater than if each element was used separately or sequentially (ADP 3-0).

1-22. Mastery of the science of tactics is necessary for leaders to understand physical and procedural constraints. These constraints include the effects from mission variables or the effects of rules of engagement on friendly and enemy force capabilities.

SOLVING TACTICAL PROBLEMS

1-23. As a part of mastering the Army profession, leaders train for various tactical situations, learn to recognize their important elements, and practice decision making under realistic conditions. They develop these abilities through years of professional military education, self-study, practical training, and operational experiences. These experiences sharpen the intuitive faculties required to solve tactical problems. Repeated deployments to similar areas require examinations of previously successful operations to stay ahead of adaptive and learning enemies.

1-24. Leaders begin developing their foundation for solving tactical problems by mastering the science of the profession. This requires them to master the use of their systems and understand methods to employ terrain to their advantage. Leaders learn to communicate their concepts of operations clearly with technically precise and doctrinally consistent verbiage, using commonly understood and accepted doctrinal terms and concepts.

1-25. Commanders apply tactics, an understanding of the situation, and judgment to create unique solutions appropriate to accomplishing the mission and the other specific mission variables. Usually several solutions exist for one problem, and some will be more effective than others. An ideal solution is decisive and postures the unit for future missions, while also providing the greatest flexibility for response to unexpected enemy actions within the higher commander's intent.

1-26. Success in tactical problem solving results from the aggressive, intelligent, and decisive use of relative combat power. *Combat power* is the total means of destructive, constructive, and information capabilities that a military unit or formation can apply at a given time (ADP 3-0). Combat power has eight elements: leadership, information, command and control, movement and maneuver, intelligence, fires, sustainment, and protection. The elements facilitate Army forces accessing joint and multinational fires and assets. The Army collectively describes the last six elements as warfighting functions. Commanders win by initiating combat on their own terms—at a time and place of their choosing—and by maintaining the initiative to make the enemy react. Commanders maintain the initiative to enable friendly forces to disrupt enemy decision making. This is particularly important during transitions between the offense and defense because retaining the initiative minimizes an enemy force's ability to react effectively to changes in friendly dispositions.

1-27. Offensive action is the key to achieving decisive results. Commanders conduct the offense to defeat enemy forces or gain control of terrain to produce the effects required by their higher commander. Circumstances may require defending; however, tactical success normally requires shifting to the offense as soon as possible. The offense ends when forces accomplish their missions, reach their limit of advance (LOA), or approach culmination. Those forces then consolidate, resume the attack, or prepare for other operations.

1-28. Commanders seek to initiate combat on the most favorable terms. Doing so allows the massing of effects against selected enemy units in vulnerable locations. Maintaining the initiative allows a commander to shift the decisive operation to exploit opportunities as they arise. Commanders seize, retain, and exploit the initiative by—

- Gaining a position of relative advantage (physical, temporal, cognitive, or virtual) over enemy forces by maneuvering more rapidly than enemy forces.
- Employing firepower to destroy critical enemy capabilities and systems.
- Conducting information operations, cyberspace operations, and electronic warfare activities to isolate and degrade enemy decision-making abilities.
- Denying enemy forces what they require for success, such as terrain, airspace, population centers, support of the population, and facilities.

- Sustaining and protecting subordinate forces before, during, and after battles.
- Maintaining a better understanding of the tactical situation than enemy forces and exploiting it.
- Planning beyond the initial operation and anticipating its branches or sequels.
- Continuously consolidating gains to defeat all forms of enemy resistance.

1-29. Momentum complements and helps maintain the initiative. Momentum reflects a unit's combat power and the velocity and tempo of its operations. Concentrating combat power at the decisive point, supported by rapid maneuver, places an enemy in a disadvantageous position. Commanders maintain focus and pressure, controlling the tempo of operations while seeking and exploiting opportunities. Maintaining momentum requires continuously assessing the situation and making risk decisions with regard to resourcing the main effort.

1-30. A thorough understanding of an operational environment greatly helps commanders to develop tactical solutions and allows them to drive the operations process. Commanders who make and implement decisions faster than a hesitant enemy, even to a small degree, gain an accruing advantage. (See ADP 6-0 for a description of the operations process.)

1-31. Transitions among operations are difficult and may create unexpected opportunities for friendly or enemy forces. Commanders and their supporting staffs quickly recognize such opportunities, acting on branches or sequels prepared during the planning process. Improvisation may be necessary to cope with unforeseen circumstances, particularly those arising from consolidating gains. *Consolidate gains* is activities to make enduring any temporary operational success and to set the conditions for a sustainable security environment, allowing for a transition of control to legitimate authorities (ADP 3-0). (See ADP 3-0 for additional information on the consolidation of gains.)

1-32. Ultimately, solutions to tactical problems result from the collective efforts of a commander's plan and the ability of subordinate leaders to execute it. Commanders are responsible for training their subordinates. The result of that rigorous and realistic training leaves commanders fully confident in their subordinates' mastery of the art and science of tactics and in their ability to execute a chosen solution.

HASTY VERSUS DELIBERATE OPERATIONS

1-33. **A *hasty operation* is an operation in which a commander directs immediately available forces, using fragmentary orders, to perform tasks with minimal preparation, trading planning and preparation time for speed of execution**. Commanders mentally synchronize the employment of available forces before issuing fragmentary orders. Hasty operations exploit the advantages of combined arms to the maximum possible extent. For example, the 9th Armored Division's seizure of the bridge at Remagen in March 1945 illustrates a hasty operation conducted with the forces immediately available. Commanders consider tangible and intangible factors, such as subordinate training levels and experience, a potential enemy reaction, time and distance, and the strengths of each subordinate and supporting unit to achieve the required degree of synchronization.

1-34. **A *deliberate operation* is an operation in which the tactical situation allows the development and coordination of detailed plans, including multiple branches and sequels**. Commanders conducting deliberate operations task-organize forces to accomplish a specific mission. That tasked combined arms team conducts extensive rehearsals and shaping operations to create the conditions for the conduct of the force's decisive operation. For example, the 1st Infantry Division's breaching operation during the opening hours of the ground phase of Operation Desert Storm in February 1991 illustrates a deliberate operation.

1-35. Most operations occur somewhere between a hasty operation and a deliberate operation. The operations process helps in the development of a common operational picture to facilitate decision making and to communicate decisions and other information between friendly forces. The sheer amount of obtainable data in the information age complicates the distinction between hasty and deliberate operations. Commanders discern intelligence from collected information to shape their decisions. Commanders who understand this nuance can focus on knowledge that enables their abilities to anticipate opportunities and build flexibility into plans.

Chapter 1

RISK

1-36. Choices and the cost of those choices characterize all operations. Commanders decide if they can accomplish their mission based on current intelligence of the enemy situation and an assessment of the assets available (including time) and the means to coordinate and synchronize those assets. If those assets are not available, commanders choose to take additional time to plan, resource, and prepare for an operation, or they articulate where and how they will assume risk.

1-37. Commanders may act on limited combat information in a time-constrained environment. *Combat information* is unevaluated data, gathered by or provided directly to the tactical commander which, due to its highly perishable nature or the criticality of the situation, cannot be processed into tactical intelligence in time to satisfy the user's tactical intelligence requirements (JP 2-01). Commanders must understand the inherent risk of acting only on combat information, since it is vulnerable to enemy deception and can be misinterpreted. The intelligence staff helps commanders assess combat information used in decision making.

1-38. Commanders cannot be successful without a willingness to act under conditions of uncertainty, which demands balancing risks with taking advantage of opportunities. No amount of intelligence can eliminate all uncertainties and inherent risks of tactical operations. Commanders will never have absolute situational understanding. A lack of information must not paralyze the decision-making process. The more information a commander collects concerning the mission variables, the better that commander is able to make informed decisions. Less information means that a commander has a greater risk of making a poor decision for a specific situation. Knowing when there is enough information to make a decision within the higher commander's intent and constraints is part of the art of tactics and is a critical skill for all leaders.

1-39. To shape success, commanders take the minimum time necessary to plan and prepare. Reduced coordination at the start of an operation may result in less than optimal effects on the enemy. However, that reduced coordination may offer increased speed and momentum and, potentially, surprise. The more time a commander takes to prepare for an operation, the more opportunity the enemy has to prepare.

1-40. Bold decisions that are adequately informed give the best promise of success. Commanders accept risk when making decisions because there will always be a degree of uncertainty. Opportunities come with risks. The willingness to accept risk is often the key to exposing enemy weaknesses. There are times when leaders cannot find ways of addressing all of the risk and should consider if the outcome is worth the risk. Situational understanding, running estimates, and planning reduces risk.

1-41. In some circumstances, commanders can forego detailed planning, extensive rehearsals, and significant changes in task organization. Their prior self-development, training, and experience allows them to assess and create overwhelming combat power at decisive points. For example, an attacking battalion task force encountering enemy security elements just moving into position can conduct actions on contact to destroy these elements without the loss of momentum. **Actions on contact are a series of combat actions, often conducted nearly simultaneously, taken on contact with the enemy to develop the situation**. Friendly commanders determine what must be done to preserve combat power and create conditions for success.

1-42. Every military decision includes risk. Commanders exercise judgement when deciding where to accept risk. As shown in figure 1-1, commanders have several techniques available to reduce the risk associated with a lack of information and intelligence in a specific operation. Some of these techniques for reducing risk require the commitment of additional resources. Deciding what resources to divert to reduce risk is part of the art of tactics. In general terms, risk is the exposure of someone or something valued to danger, harm, or loss. Risk is an expression of the probability and implications of an activity or event, with positive or negative consequences taking place. It is a measure of the likelihood of something going right or wrong, and the associated impact, good or bad.

1-43. Because risk is part of every operation, it cannot be avoided. Commanders analyze risk in collaboration with subordinates to help determine what level of risk exists and how to mitigate it. When considering how much risk to accept with a COA, commanders consider risk to the force and risk to the mission against the perceived benefit. They apply judgment with regard to the importance of an objective, time available, and anticipated cost. Commanders need to balance the tension between creating opportunities, protecting the force, and accepting and managing risks that must be taken to accomplish their mission.

1-44. While each situation is different, commanders avoid undue caution or commitment of resources to guard against every perceived threat. An unrealistic expectation of avoiding all risk is detrimental to mission accomplishment. Waiting for perfect intelligence and synchronization increases risk or closes a window of opportunity. Successful operations require commanders and subordinates to manage accepted risk, exercise initiative, and act decisively even when the outcome is uncertain.

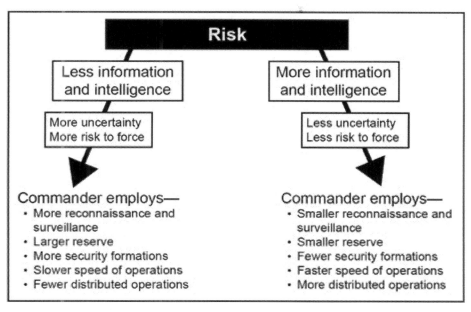

Figure 1-1. Risk reduction factors

1-45. Commanders—when supported by systems that can access current and accurate information—exploit their understanding of the enemy and friendly situations. This understanding allows maneuver at favorable ranges and ensures responsive and flexible support of forces. The integration of information technologies, capable leaders, and agile formations reduces risk and facilitates decisive action.

1-46. Risk reduction does not always mean seeking to increase information about the enemy at the expense of time. Commanders partially compensate for this gap by maintaining flexibility in their troop dispositions. They accomplish this by increasing the depth of their unit security areas; the size, number, capabilities of their security elements; and the size of their reserve. **A *security area* is that area occupied by a unit's security elements and includes the areas of influence of those security elements**. Commanders choose formations that provide versatility and allow for initial enemy contact with the smallest possible friendly force. Another way to compensate for increased risk is to provide additional time and resources for subordinate elements to develop the situation before committing to a particular COA.

1-47. Friendly force agility further mitigates risk in tactical operations. Agility is the ability of friendly forces to react faster than enemy forces. It is as much a mental as a physical quality. Agility permits the rapid concentration of friendly strengths against enemy vulnerabilities. Friendly forces achieve agility through rigorous and realistic training, well-known and drilled unit standard operating procedures, maintained and continuously shared understanding and estimates, and the use of the mission command approach.

1-48. In any operation, the relationship among information, uncertainty, risk, size of reserves and security forces, and the disposition of the main body may frequently changes. **The *main body* is the principal part of a tactical command or formation. It does not include detached elements of the command, such as advance guards, flank guards, and covering forces**. Commanders continually weigh the balance of information, uncertainty, risk, and size of reserves and security forces against the disposition of the main body. They then make adjustments as needed.

1-49. Changes to task organization, mission, and priorities are part of the operations process. Commanders, advised by their staffs, determine the optimal formation and organization for a specific mission, and they continuously assess risk. If the situation warrants, commanders make appropriate changes and allocate resources to minimize risk through these changes. Every change has opportunities and risks. Commanders balance the two to achieve their purpose.

Chapter 2
Common Tactical Concepts and Echelons

Tacticians apply common tactical concepts, military definitions, and the tactical echelons and organizations as they conduct offensive and defensive operations. This chapter discusses joint interdependence, principles of joint operations, and the operational and mission variables. It introduces the Army doctrinal hierarchy that forms the framework that organizes this publication and its subordinate publications as well as warfighting functions and defeat mechanisms. This chapter contains a discussion of common tactical concepts and echelons. This chapter concludes by covering forms of maneuver, forms or defense, and echelons.

JOINT INTERDEPENDENCE

2-1. Army forces conduct offensive and defensive operations as members of an interdependent joint force, applying land power as part of unified action. Joint interdependence is the purposeful reliance by one Service on another Service to complement and reinforce each other's effects. Joint capabilities enhance the effectiveness of Army forces. Joint operations also have interagency and multinational aspects. (See JP-1, JP 3-0, and ADP 3-0 for additional information on joint interdependence. See JP 3-08 and FM 3-16 for information on Army interagency and multinational aspects.)

Principles of Joint Operations
Objective
Offensive
Mass
Maneuver
Economy of force
Unity of command
Security
Surprise
Simplicity
Restraint
Perseverance
Legitimacy

PRINCIPLES OF JOINT OPERATIONS

2-2. JP 3-0 defines the twelve principles of joint operations and provides general guidance for conducting military operations. The joint principles originate from Army doctrine. First published in America in 1923 as general principles in *Field Service Regulations United States Army*, the first nine, as principles of war, have stood the tests of time, analysis, experimentation, and practice. The principles of joint operations provide a crucial link between pure theory and actual application. (See JP 3-0 for further information on these principles.)

OPERATIONAL VARIABLES

2-3. Army planners use the operational variables to describe an operational environment. Operational variables are those aspects of an operational environment which affect operations, and they differ from one area of operations to another. Army planners analyze an operational environment in terms of eight interrelated operational variables: political, military, economic, social, information, infrastructure, physical environment, and time (also known as PMESII-PT). As soon as a commander and staff have an indication of where their unit may deploy, they begin analyzing that location's operational environment using the operational variables. They continue to refine and update their analysis even after receiving a mission and throughout the course of the ensuing operation. (See ADP 3-0 for additional information on the operational variables.)

Operational Variables
Political
Military
Economic
Social
Information
Infrastructure
Physical Environment
Time

Chapter 2

MISSION VARIABLES

2-4. Upon receipt of a mission, Army leaders filter relevant information categorized by the operational variables into the categories of the mission variables for use during mission analysis. Incorporating an analysis of the operational variables with the mission variables ensures Army leaders understand the context in which they perform their missions.

2-5. The mission variables describe the conditions in which commanders and staffs execute the art and science of tactics. An analysis of these mission variables is critical during the military decision-making process. Commanders consider each variable during the operations process. (See ADP 3-0 for additional information on the mission variables.)

Mission Variables
Mission
Enemy
Terrain and weather
Troops and support available
Time available
Civil considerations

THE ARMY'S TACTICAL DOCTRINAL TAXONOMY

2-6. Figure 2-1 shows the taxonomy of the Army's tactical doctrine for the four elements of decisive action and their subordinate operations or tasks. While an operation's primary element is offense, defense, stability, or defense support of civil authorities, different units involved in that operation may be conducting different types and subordinate variations of operations. Commanders rapidly shift emphasis from one element to another to maintain tempo and keep enemy forces off balance. Maintaining tempo and flexibility through transitions contributes to successful operations.

2-7. Commanders perform enabling operations to help in the planning, preparation, and execution of any of the four elements of decisive action. Enabling operations are never decisive operations. Commanders use enabling operations to complement current operations or to transition between phases or element of decisive action.

2-8. The tactical mission tasks listed at the bottom of figure 2-1 describe both actions and purposes. The tactical mission tasks have specific military definitions different from those found in common English. (See FM 3-90-1 for detailed information on individual tactical mission tasks listed in figure 2-1.)

2-9. The elements of decisive action are not discrete, mutually exclusive operations. Tactical missions can contain elements of the offense, defense, and stability or defense support of civil authorities. The lower the echelon, the less a formation can focus on more than one of the elements. During large-scale combat operations, it is unlikely that units performing close combat also conduct stability tasks.

WARFIGHTING FUNCTIONS

2-10. A *warfighting function* is a group of tasks and systems united by a common purpose that commanders use to accomplish missions and training objectives (ADP 3-0). The warfighting functions provide an intellectual organization of common capabilities available to commanders and staffs to achieve objectives and accomplish missions. In 2008, the Army established six warfighting functions that linked to the joint functions established in JP 3-0. The Army defines each of these six warfighting functions:

- The *command and control warfighting function* is the related tasks and a system that enable commanders to synchronize and converge all elements of combat power (ADP 3-0).
- The *movement and maneuver warfighting function* is the related tasks and systems that move and employ forces to achieve a position of relative advantage over the enemy and other threats (ADP 3-0). Direct fire and close combat are inherent in maneuver.
- The *intelligence warfighting function* is the related tasks and systems that facilitate understanding the enemy, terrain, weather, civil considerations, and other significant aspects of the operational environment (ADP 3-0).
- The *fires warfighting function* is the related tasks and systems that create and converge effects in all domains against the adversary or enemy to enable operations across the range of military operations (ADP 3-0).

Common Tactical Concepts and Echelons

- The *sustainment warfighting function* is the related tasks and systems that provide support and services to ensure freedom of action, extend operational reach, and prolong endurance (ADP 3-0).
- The *protection warfighting function* is the related tasks and systems that preserve the force so the commander can apply maximum combat power to accomplish the mission (ADP 3-0).

The successful execution of operations requires the use of all the warfighting functions in various combinations and with the other two elements of combat power—leadership and information.

Elements of Decisive Action

Offensive operations
- Movement to Contact
  - Search and Attack
  - Cordon and Search
- Attack
  - Ambush
  - Counterattack
  - Demonstration
  - Feint
  - Raid
  - Spoiling attack
- Exploitation
- Pursuit
  - Frontal
  - Combination

Defensive operations
- Area Defense
- Mobile Defense
- Retrograde
  - Delay
  - Withdraw
  - Retirement

Stability operations tasks
- Establish civil security
- Support to civil control
- Restore essential services
- Support to governance
- Support to economic and infrastructure development
- Conduct security cooperation

Defensive support of civil authorities tasks
- Provide support for Domestic disasters
- Provide support for domestic chemical, biological, radiological, and nuclear incidents
- Provide support for domestic civilian law enforcement agencies
- Provide other designated domestic support

Enabling operations

- **Reconnaissance**
  - Area
  - Reconnaissance in force
  - Route
  - Special
  - Zone
- **Passage of lines**
  - Forward
  - Rearward
- **Troop movement**
  - Administrative movement
  - Approach march
  - Tactical road march
- **Relief in place**
  - Sequential
  - Simultaneous
  - Staggered
- **Security**
  - Screen
  - Guard
  - Cover
  - Area

Tactical Mission Tasks

- Ambush
- Attack by fire
- Block
- Breach
- Bypass
- Canalize
- Clear
- Contain
- Control
- Counterreconnaisance
- Destroy
- Defeat
- Disengagement
- Disrupt
- Exfiltrate
- Fix
- Follow and assume
- Follow and support
- Interdict
- Isolate
- Neutralize
- Occupy
- Reduce
- Retain
- Secure
- Seize
- Support by fire
- Suppress
- Turn

Forms of Maneuver and Forms of the Defense

- Envelopment
- Frontal assault
- Infiltration
- Penetration
- Turning movement

- Defense of a linear obstacle
- Perimeter defense
- Reverse slope defense

Figure 2-1. Taxonomy of Army tactics

Chapter 2

DEFEAT MECHANISMS

2-11. A *defeat mechanism* is a method through which friendly forces accomplish their mission against enemy opposition (ADP 3-0). Tactical forces at all echelons use combinations of the four defeat mechanisms: destroy, dislocate, disintegrate, and isolate. There are also stability mechanisms used in the conduct of stability. (See ADP 3-0 for a discussion of both defeat and stability mechanisms.)

BASIC TACTICAL CONCEPTS

2-12. Paragraphs 2-13 through 2-79 discuss the basic tactical concepts common to both the offense and defense. These concepts—along with the principles of joint operations, the mission variables, operational design, warfighting functions, running estimates, input from other commanders, and their own experience and judgment—allow commanders to articulate their concept of operations.

> **Basic Tactical Concepts**
> Area of influence
> Area of interest
> Area of operations
> Avenue of approach
> Combined arms
> Committed force
> Concept of operations
> Decisive engagement
> Defeat in detail
> Economy of force
> Encirclement
> Engagement area
> Flanks
> Forms of contact
> Local security
> Maneuver
> Meeting engagement
> Movement
> Mutual support
> Operation
> Operational framework
> Piecemeal commitment
> Reconstitution
> Reserve
> Rules of engagement
> Supporting distance
> Supporting range
> Tactical mobility
> Uncommitted forces
> Weight the decisive operation

AREA OF INFLUENCE

2-13. An *area of influence* is a geographical area wherein a commander is directly capable of influencing operations by maneuver or fire support systems normally under the commander's command or control (JP 3-0). Understanding an area of influence helps commanders and staffs identify the broader effects of operations and branches to the current plan. Commanders collaborate to define AOs to match a unit's area of influence. An AO that is too large for a unit to control provides an enemy force with maneuver space or depletes a commander's combat power. If an area of influence differs in size from its assigned AO, commanders or appropriate staff officers—

- Change the dispositions of available current systems to match the size of an area of influence and ensure coverage of key areas, installations, and systems.
- Request additional assets.
- Request boundary adjustments to reduce the size of an AO.
- Communicate the increased risk and use economy of force measures.
- Adjust a unit's area of influence by phases to encompass an entire AO.

AREA OF INTEREST

2-14. An *area of interest* is that area of concern to the commander, including the area of influence, areas adjacent thereto, and extending into enemy territory (JP 3-0). This area also includes areas occupied by enemy forces who could jeopardize the accomplishment of the mission. Typically, a commander's area of interest is much larger than that commander's AO. Depending on the type and scale of an operation, the size of an assigned area of interest varies.

AREA OF OPERATIONS

2-15. An *area of operations* is an operational area defined by a commander for land and maritime forces that should be large enough to accomplish their missions and protect their forces (JP 3-0). The joint force land component commander, Army Service component command commander, or Army forces commander assigns subordinates AOs. Those subordinates further assign AOs from their assigned AO, down to the battalion or company echelon based on the mission variables. A unit assigned an AO may not change control measures imposed by a higher echelon headquarters within its AO. However, it may establish additional control measures to coordinate and synchronize its operations. Assigning an AO to a subordinate headquarters decentralizes execution by empowering subordinate commanders to use their own initiative to accomplish their missions. (See ADP 6-0 for more information on AO assignment.)

2-16. Commanders normally assign AOs to subordinate maneuver units, such as brigade combat teams (BCTs) or maneuver enhancement brigades. Assigning an AO both restricts and facilitates the movement of units and use of fires. It restricts those units not assigned responsibility for an AO from moving through other AOs. It also restricts outside units from firing into an AO or allowing the effects of their fires to affect the AO. Coordination with the unit assigned the AO relieves some of these restrictions.

2-17. All units assigned an AO have the following responsibilities within the boundaries of that AO:
- Terrain management.
- Information collection
- Civil-military operations.
- Movement control.
- Clearance of fires.
- Security.
- Personnel recovery.
- Airspace control of assigned airspace.
- Minimum-essential stability tasks.
- Environmental considerations, if applicable.

2-18. The organizational design of the three types of BCTs and the maneuver enhancement brigade allows them to be assigned AOs. If commanders assign an AO to a unit that is not designed to perform all the tasks associated with controlling an AO, they clearly articulate which AO responsibilities they will not perform and what risk the commander is willing to assume. They also designate the units or command posts that perform those functions on their behalf.

Terrain Management

2-19. **Terrain management is the process of allocating terrain by establishing areas of operations, designating assembly areas, and specifying locations for units and activities to deconflict activities that might interfere with each other**. Commanders assigned AOs are responsible for terrain management within the boundaries of those AOs. Throughout operations, commanders manage terrain within their boundaries by assigning subordinate units areas and positions. Their command posts track unit locations and movements and adjust control measures to deconflict space and control movements within their AOs. A higher echelon headquarters may dictate that another unit position itself within a subordinate unit's AO. The commander assigned the AO retains approval authority for that unit's placement. This ensures that the commander controlling the AO knows what units are in the AO and where they are located. This allows commanders to synchronize efforts. As tenants of an AO, units are required to coordinate with the headquarters assigned the AO.

Information Collection

2-20. Within their AOs, commanders perform intelligence, surveillance, and reconnaissance (known as ISR) as part of their collection efforts. They perform these tasks and conduct operations to maintain current and accurate common operational pictures of their AOs. They share the common operational picture with higher echelon, adjacent, subordinate, and tenant units to maintain a clear understanding of their AOs and areas of interest.

2-21. *Intelligence operations* are the tasks undertaken by military intelligence units through the intelligence disciplines to obtain information to satisfy validated requirements (ADP 2-0). Intelligence operations collect information about the activities and resources of the threat or information concerning the characteristics of an operational environment. The intelligence disciplines of counterintelligence, geospatial intelligence, human intelligence, measurement and signature intelligence, signals intelligence, and technical intelligence routinely perform tasks associated with intelligence operations. (See FM 2-0 for additional information on intelligence operations.)

Chapter 2

2-22. The Army views the intelligence process as a model that describes how the intelligence warfighting function facilitates situational understanding and supports decision making. Commanders and staffs must understand the intelligence process. To be effective, collected data and information require processing, timely analysis, fusion, distribution, and access. The Army intelligence process consists of four steps (plan and direct, collect and process, produce, and disseminate) and two continuing activities (analyze and assess). (See ADP 2-0 for additional information on the intelligence process.)

2-23. Surveillance is a systematic collection of information. It should be continuous, and it involves active and passive activities. Reconnaissance is the active collection of information, and it usually includes human participation. Both surveillance and reconnaissance produce combat information that meets one or more of the commander's critical information requirements or intelligence requirements. (See chapter 5 for additional information on reconnaissance operations. See FM 3-90-2 for a detailed discussion of reconnaissance.)

2-24. **Security operations are those operations performed by commanders to provide early and accurate warning of enemy operations, to provide the forces being protected with time and maneuver space within which to react to the enemy, and to develop the situation to allow commanders to effectively use their protected forces**. Security operations and reconnaissance operations differ in that security operations focus on the protected force or location while reconnaissance operations focus on the enemy and terrain. (See chapter 5 for additional information on security operations.)

Civil-Military Operations

2-25. *Civil-military operations* is activities of a commander performed by designated military forces that establish, maintain, influence, or exploit relations between military forces and indigenous populations and institutions by directly supporting the achievement of objectives relating to the reestablishment or maintenance of stability within a region or host nation (JP 3-57). Commanders conduct civil-military operations to coordinate and integrate joint, single-Service, and multinational operations with the operations of other U.S. government departments and agencies, nongovernmental organizations, intergovernmental organizations (for example, the United Nations), and the private sector.

Movement Control

2-26. *Movement control* is the dual process of committing allocated transportation assets and regulating movements according to command priorities to synchronize distribution flow over lines of communications to sustain land forces (ADP 4-0). Units transiting another unit's AO are required to coordinate with that unit's headquarters. Generally, the unit assigned an AO controls movement within that AO. The designation, maintenance, route security, and control of movement along routes within an AO are the responsibility of the owning unit unless the higher echelon coordinating instructions directs otherwise. The commander of an AO may designate movement routes as open, supervised, dispatch, reserved, or prohibited. Each route's designation varies based on the mission variables. (See ATP 4-16 for a discussion of movement planning and control measures.)

Clearance of Fires

2-27. *Clearance of fires* is the process by which the supported commander ensures that fires or their effects will have no unintended consequences on friendly units or the scheme of maneuver (FM 3-09). The commander of the AO clears fires. Within their AO, units may employ most direct or indirect fire systems without receiving further clearance from their higher echelon headquarters. However, there are three exceptions. The first and most common exception is that a unit may not use munitions within its own AO without coordination if the effects of those munitions extend beyond its AO. Second, a higher echelon headquarters may explicitly restrict the use of certain munitions, such as scatterable mines. Third, a higher echelon headquarters may impose a restrictive fire support coordination measure (FSCM), such as a no-fire area around a dislocated civilian camp.

2-28. Generally, a commander may not employ indirect fires across boundaries without receiving clearance from the unit into whose AO the fires enter. In limited circumstances, commanders use direct and observed joint fires when firing across boundaries at positively identified enemy forces when there is no time to coordinate with adjacent friendly units.

Common Tactical Concepts and Echelons

2-29. A *fire support coordination measure* is a measure employed by commanders to facilitate the rapid engagement of targets and simultaneously provide safeguards for friendly forces (JP 3-0). FSCMs govern the employment of artillery and mortars, attacks by Army rotary-wing aircraft, fires from unmanned aircraft, and close air support and air interdiction by fixed-wing aircraft. FSCMs enhance the rapid engagement of targets; protect forces, populations, critical infrastructure, and sites of religious or cultural significance; and shape future operations. Commanders position and adjust FSCMs consistent with the situation and after consulting higher, subordinate, supporting, and affected commanders.

2-30. FSCMs can be either permissive or restrictive in nature. Permissive FSCMs are the coordinated fire line, fire support coordination line (FSCL), free-fire area, and the kill box. Restrictive FSCMs are the no-fire area, restrictive fire area, restrictive fire line, fire support area and fire support station, and zone of fire. There are additional target acquisition control measures and airspace coordinating measures that impact the clearance of fires, such as critical friendly zones, call for fire zones, artillery target intelligence zones, sensor zones, airspace coordination areas, coordinating altitudes, and restricted operations areas. (See FM 3-09 for the definition of each of these FSCMs and a discussion of each use.)

Security

2-31. The general security of all units operating within an AO is the responsibility of the unit assigned the AO. Unit commanders remain responsible for their unit's local security. Commanders assigned AOs assess risk and perform security operations. The conduct of security operations prevents surprise and provides time for units located within an AO to respond to enemy actions. When commanders cannot or choose not to provide security measures throughout their AO, they specify what they are not providing and then coordinate with adjacent, subordinate, and tenant units.

Personnel Recovery

2-32. *Army personnel recovery* is the military efforts taken to prepare for and execute the recovery and reintegration of isolated personnel (FM 3-50). Isolation occurs through enemy action, disorientation, or environmental conditions. The commander assigned an AO is responsible for recovering and returning isolated persons within that AO to friendly control. Large-scale combat operations require an analysis of the mission variable before triggering an immediate response. If immediate recovery is not undertaken or is not successful, the unit conducts detailed planning and executes deliberate recovery. Army forces support external supported recovery of joint task force components, interagency organizations, and multinational forces. (See FM 3-50 for additional information on Army personnel recovery and the operations process.)

Airspace Control of Assigned Airspace

2-33. *Airspace control* is capabilities and procedures used to increase operational effectiveness by promoting the safe, efficient, and flexible use of airspace (JP 3-52). The division joint air-ground integration center (JAGIC)—composed of the Army's fires cell, air missile defense cell, airspace element, and USAF's air support operations center and tactical air control party—executes airspace control responsibilities for division-assigned airspace when the division headquarters serves as tactical headquarters and is assigned a volume of airspace by the airspace control authority. The division airspace element coordinates with the Army battlefield coordination detachment's airspace section. If the division is the senior Army headquarters, this element ensures the joint airspace policies and documents incorporate the Army airspace priorities and requirements. The division is normally a tactical headquarters subordinate to a tactical corps or a joint force land component. In this case, the airspace element provides airspace requirements to the higher headquarters' airspace section for integration into its airspace plan. (See paragraph 2-35 for more information on the division airspace element.) This integration applies to the next airspace control order and the higher echelon headquarters' airspace control appendix. (See ATP 3-92 for more information on the airspace element's responsibilities when the division is an operational headquarters.)

2-34. The airspace element is the airspace functional lead for the division staff. Airspace element personnel integrate airspace operations with the functional and integrating cells through the airspace control working group. The tactical air control party and the air support operations center (known as ASOC) are co-located with the division headquarters; they are also part of the airspace control working group. The airspace element develops standard operating procedures and airspace control annexes that help standardize airspace control operations among subordinate units. These procedures and annexes ensure consistency with joint airspace procedures, the theater airspace control plan, aeronautical information publications, and associated plans and orders. To support the division mission, the airspace elements are responsible for—

- Providing airspace control expertise for the commander.
- Monitoring joint airspace operations.
- Planning and updating input to the joint airspace control plan.
- Integrating the airspace control architecture into the joint airspace control architecture.
- Developing the airspace control architecture to support plans.
- Drafting all airspace control input for operation orders, operation plans, appendices, and running estimates.
- Planning and requesting airspace coordinating measures.
- Deconflicting airspace through the appropriate authority.
- Coordinating with the movement and maneuver (for aviation), intelligence (for information collection), and fires and protection (for air and missile defense) cells.
- Providing air traffic service expertise to the headquarters.

2-35. The division airspace element oversees airspace control for all of the division's assigned airspace. When a division allocates part of its AO to a subordinate brigade, it delegates some airspace management responsibilities to that brigade. However, the division airspace element still integrates airspace users over the entire division AO. If the division has an unusually large AO or if the division AO is noncontiguous, then it can delegate more airspace control responsibilities to subordinate units. Normally, delegation of airspace control for unified action partner airspace requires significant augmentation of the brigade with organized, trained, and equipped airspace control personnel from both the Army and the Air Force.

Division and Corps Airspace Management

2-36. If required, the division headquarters provides airspace control to support multinational forces under the operational control of the division. If these forces lack airspace control capabilities, they require assistance from the division airspace element. They receive support similar to Army functional brigades working directly for the division. Airspace elements provide airspace control subject matter expertise for planning. Airspace planning focuses on near-real-time airspace control during a mission and provides commanders flexibility while reducing risk.

2-37. The United States Air Force aligns air support operations center capabilities with Army divisions. Aligning air support operations centers provides an effective method to command and control close air support, intelligence, surveillance, reconnaissance, and air interdiction operations. Aligning air support operations centers also provides an effective means to coordinate suppression of enemy air defense in division-assigned airspace.

2-38. Army airspace planners at the senior operational and tactical levels help to develop the joint airspace control plan. Their participation is critical if they intend to request the authority to control division-assigned airspace using the JAGIC technique. (See ATP 3-91.1 for a description of these functions.) As shown in figure 2-2, division-assigned airspace is airspace in which the airspace control authority delegated the responsibility for control of that airspace to the division, in accordance with the airspace control plan and airspace control order. Division-assigned airspace is assigned by the airspace control authority and is normally that airspace between the rear boundary and the FSCL, between the lateral boundaries up to the coordinating altitude. The *coordinating altitude* is airspace coordinating measure that uses altitude to separate users and as the transition between different airspace control elements (JP 3-52). This delegation of authorities does not include authorities vested in the area air defense commander. A JAGIC-enabled division is manned and equipped to control procedurally the tactical airspace over the division AO, within division-assigned airspace. The *coordination level* is a procedural method to separate fixed- and rotary-wing aircraft by determining an altitude below which fixed-wing aircraft normally will not fly (JP 3-52).

Common Tactical Concepts and Echelons

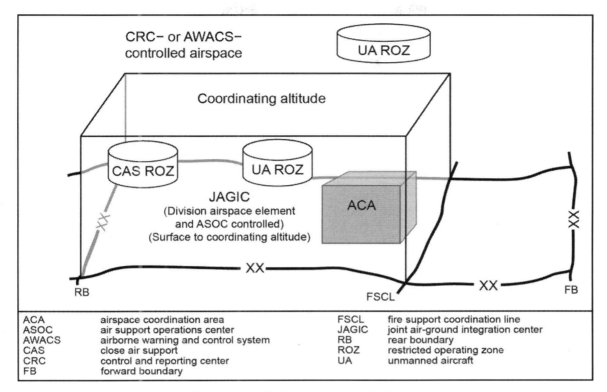

Figure 2-2. Division-assigned airspace

2-39. Army commanders and staffs use positive control methods (division positive control is limited to areas controlled by Army or joint air traffic control elements), procedural control methods (used throughout division-assigned airspace), or a combination of both methods. When a division is delegated control of airspace, the JAGIC controls division-assigned airspace using primarily procedural control. The airmen in the JAGIC may provide procedural control for joint force air component command aircraft operating in the division-assigned airspace. The airspace control appendix specifies control for division aircraft. (See FM 6-0 for orders annexes. See paragraph 3a of appendix 10 to Annex C, *Operations*.) Normally the JAGIC relies on the BCTs to integrate division aviation elements operating below the coordinating altitude in their AO. Simultaneously, the JAGIC airspace Soldiers integrate division aircraft operating above the coordinating altitude and any division aircraft operating in parts of the division AO not further assigned as a brigade AO. For example, during a division deep operation the JAGIC is the airspace control agency for Shadow or Gray Eagle unmanned aircraft within division-assigned airspace as well as for aircraft operating forward of one or more BCT AOs.

Brigade Airspace Management

2-40. BCTs and maneuver enhancement brigades are only capable of and, when designated, responsible for, airspace management of Army airspace users within their AO. The authority of these brigades over unified action partner airspace users varies and is specified in the higher echelon headquarters airspace control appendix. All Army airspace users transiting a brigade AO coordinate with the brigade responsible for the AO they are transiting. A division only integrates Army airspace use between brigades if adjudication between brigades is necessary. Brigades normally contact the United States Air Force air support operations center or JAGIC as the joint airspace element controlling airspace over a brigade's AO.

2-41. The division with responsibilities for some airspace tasks may task brigades without an organic air defense airspace management (or brigade aviation element), but, like any other BCT, those brigades rely on their higher echelon headquarters for complete airspace control. If a functional brigade falls under the tactical or operational control of a BCT or maneuver enhancement brigade, the BCT or maneuver enhancement brigade integrates the functional brigade's airspace requirements. If a functional brigade falls directly under

Chapter 2

the control of a corps or division, then the corps or division airspace element integrates the functional brigade airspace requirements.

2-42. Most multifunctional support brigades do not routinely control AOs but conduct operations throughout a corps or division AO. Normally these brigades coordinate their airspace use with the divisions and brigades that have AOs. Airspace control becomes more complex when a corps tasks these multifunctional support brigades to accomplish a mission that affects airspace use in other AOs. The multifunctional support brigade conducting the operation submits its airspace requirements with the higher echelon headquarters airspace element providing planning and airspace control support to the multifunctional support brigade's air defense airspace management element. The division airspace element checks that it adjusts the airspace plan to account for the multifunctional support brigade commander's priorities and concept of operations.

Minimum-Essential Stability Tasks

2-43. Combat places civilians in harm's way. It often affects their access to necessary items, such as food, water, shelter, and emergency medical care. Generally, the responsibility for providing the basic needs of the people within a unit's AO rests with their government or designated civil authorities, agencies, and organizations. Individual families, private commercial companies, and corporations also provide many of these goods and services. Unit plans for combat operations address the provision of minimum-essential stability tasks—providing civil security, food, water, shelter, and emergency medical treatment—to civilians located within their AO in accordance with the laws of war and international standards. Unit commanders balance the provision of those minimum-essential stability tasks with their capability to conduct the offense or defense. Units address area security and the six primary stability tasks as practical until they can transfer responsibility for those tasks to another organization. The six primary stability tasks are—

- Establish civil security.
- Establish civil control.
- Restore essential services.
- Support governance.
- Support economic and infrastructure development.
- Conduct security cooperation.

2-44. Commanders request the resources they need to perform stability tasks for their assigned AO. If the requirements exceed their organization's capacity, they request additional or follow-on forces to provide additional resources. Commanders at all levels assess resources available against their missions to determine how best to ensure minimum-essential stability tasks are performed. (See ATP 3-07.5 for more information on stability tasks.)

Environmental Considerations

2-45. Commanders have the responsibility to integrate environmental considerations into planning and operations if applicable. Commanders use judgment in determining how environmental considerations affect their units (either actively or passively) when conducting operations. Responsibility for environmental issues is not included in the list of responsibilities associated with a unit assigned an AO in ADP 3-0. However, environmental considerations do apply in one degree or another to all units. Environmental considerations most significantly affect units consolidating gains or remaining in a location for an extended time. (See ATP 3-34.5 for additional information on environmental considerations.)

AVENUE OF APPROACH

2-46. **An *avenue of approach* is a path used by an attacking force leading to its objective or to key terrain. Avenues of approach exist in all domains**. Effective commanders identify avenues of approach since all COAs that involve maneuver depend on available avenues of approach. While conducting the offense, commanders evaluate avenues of approach in terms of their ability to facilitate friendly maneuver to the objective and the enemy force's capability to affect the objective. Conversely, while conducting the defense, commanders analyze avenues of approach in terms of their ability to facilitate an enemy force's attack on friendly positions and the capability of friendly forces to reinforce the battle area.

COMBINED ARMS

2-47. As defined in paragraph 1-21, combined arms includes all capabilities made available to a commander from joint, multinational, interagency, intergovernmental, nongovernmental, and private volunteer organizations. Weapons and units work more effectively when they operate together. No single action, weapon, branch, or warfighting function generates sufficient power by itself to achieve the effects required to prevail.

COMMITTED FORCE

2-48. **A *committed force* is a force in contact with an enemy or deployed on a specific mission or course of action, which precludes its employment elsewhere.** A force with an on-order mission is considered a committed force.

CONCEPT OF OPERATIONS

2-49. The *concept of operations* is a statement that directs the manner in which subordinate units cooperate to accomplish the mission and establishes the sequence of actions the force will use to achieve the end state (ADP 5-0). The concept of operations expands on the commander's intent by describing how the commander wants the force to accomplish the mission. The concept of operations promotes general understanding by stating the task that directly accomplishes the mission and the units that will execute it. (See ADP 5-0 for additional information.)

DECISIVE ENGAGEMENT

2-50. **A *decisive engagement* is an engagement in which a unit is considered fully committed and cannot maneuver or extricate itself.** In the absence of outside assistance, an action must be fought to a conclusion with the forces available. A unit's mission may result in the unit fighting a decisive engagement, such as when it is tasked to hold key terrain. A unit is considered to be decisively engaged when it is fully committed to that engagement.

DEFEAT IN DETAIL

2-51. ***Defeat in detail* is concentrating overwhelming combat power against separate parts of a force rather than defeating the entire force at once.** A smaller force can use this technique to achieve success against a larger enemy. Defeat in detail can occur sequentially or separately. For example, a commander can mass overwhelming combat power effects against an enemy element outside the supporting distance of the rest of the enemy force to defeat the enemy element before it can be reinforced.

ECONOMY OF FORCE

2-52. *Economy of force* is the judicious employment and distribution of forces so as to expend the minimum essential combat power on secondary efforts to allocate the maximum possible combat power on primary efforts (JP 3-0). It is a principle of war. Commanders employ economy of force measures (and assume risk) to expend minimum essential combat power on their shaping operations or supporting efforts to provide the maximum possible combat power for their decisive operation or main effort.

ENCIRCLEMENT OPERATIONS

2-53. ***Encirclement operations* are operations where one force loses its freedom of maneuver because an opposing force is able to isolate it by controlling all ground lines of communications and reinforcement.** A unit can conduct offensive encirclement operations to isolate an enemy force or conduct defensive encirclement operations because of the unit's isolation from the actions of an enemy force. (For more information on encirclement operations, see FM 3-90-2.)

ENGAGEMENT AREA

2-54. Some situations, such as engaging enemy forces from battle positions, have the best choice for control being to sub-divide an engagement area. In this instance, subordinate units operate in the AO of their higher headquarters. **An *engagement area* is an area where the commander intends to contain and destroy an enemy force with the massed effects of all available weapons and supporting systems.**

FLANKS

2-55. **A *flank* is the right or left limit of a unit**. For a stationary unit, flanks are designated in terms of an enemy's actual or expected location. For a moving unit, the direction of movement defines the flanks. Commanders try to deny an enemy the opportunity to engage their flanks because a unit cannot concentrate as much direct fire on its flanks as it can to the front. Commanders seek to engage the flanks of enemy units for the same reason. (Figures 2-3 and 2-4 depict flanks of a stationary and a moving unit.)

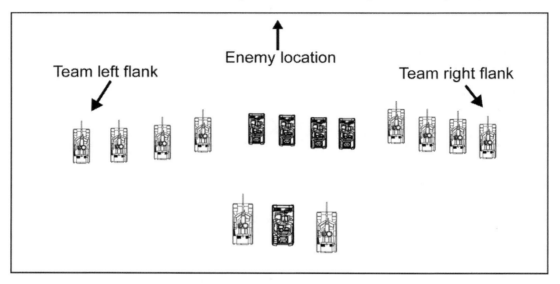

Figure 2-3. Flanks of a stationary unit

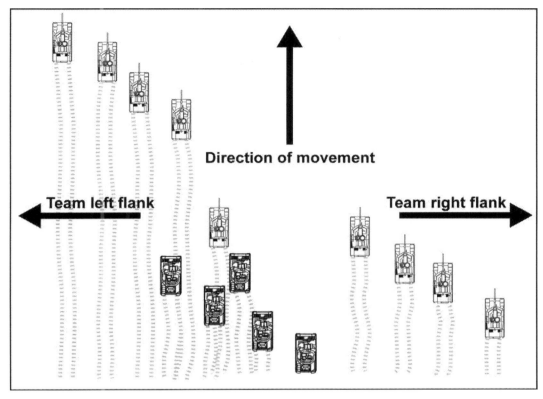

Figure 2-4. Flanks of a moving unit

2-56. Commanders try to deny enemy forces opportunities to engage the rear of friendly forces. They seek to engage the rear of enemy forces because it is difficult for enemy forces to concentrate direct fires to their rear without a significant redeployment of assets.

2-57. **An *assailable flank* is a flank exposed to attack or envelopment**. An exposed flank usually results from the terrain, the weakness of forces, the technical capability of an opponent, or a gap between adjacent units. Sufficient room must exist for the attacking force to maneuver for the flank to be assailable. A unit may not have an assailable flank if both flanks link into other forces. When a unit has an assailable flank, the commander may attempt to protect it by using various techniques, such as planning and preparing supplementary positions.

2-58. **A *flanking position* is a geographical location on the flank of a force from which effective fires can be placed on that flank**. An attacking commander maneuvers to occupy flanking positions against a defending force to place destructive fires directly on enemy vulnerabilities. A defending commander maneuvers to occupy positions on an attacking force's flanks for the same reason.

FORMS OF CONTACT

2-59. There are eight forms of contact: visual; direct; indirect; non-hostile; obstacles; aircraft; chemical, biological, radiological, and nuclear (CBRN); and electronic. (Electronic contact includes contact in cyberspace.) Units may experience all forms of contact simultaneously. Leaders always assume that they are in contact with peer threats, particularly electronic contact.

LOCAL SECURITY

2-60. ***Local security* is the low-level security activities conducted near a unit to prevent surprise by the enemy**. Local security is closely associated with unit force protection efforts. Local security provides immediate protection to the friendly force.

Chapter 2

MANEUVER

2-61. *Maneuver* is the employment of forces in the operational area, through movement in combination with fires and information, to achieve a position of advantage in respect to the enemy (JP 3-0). For the Army, **maneuver is movement in conjunction with fires**. A *position of relative advantage* is a location or the establishment of a favorable condition within the area of operations that provides the commander with temporary freedom of action to enhance combat power over an enemy or influence the enemy to accept risk and move to a position of disadvantage (ADP 3-0). It is possible for this position of relative advantage to exist in any or all the dimensions of the information environment—physical, informational, and cognitive. Maneuver creates and exposes enemy vulnerabilities to the massed effects of friendly combat power. A commander employs elements of combat power in symmetrical and asymmetrical ways to attain positional advantages over an enemy force and then exploits those positions of relative advantage.

MEETING ENGAGEMENT

2-62. **A *meeting engagement* is a combat action that occurs when a moving force, incompletely deployed for battle, engages an enemy at an unexpected time and place**. A friendly force can encounter a stationary or moving enemy force. A meeting engagement does not require both forces be surprised. The force making unexpected contact is the one conducting a meeting engagement. Such encounters often occur in small-unit operations when reconnaissance has been ineffective. The force that reacts first to the unexpected contact generally gains an advantage over its enemy.

2-63. A meeting engagement may also occur when opponents are aware of each other and both decide to attack to obtain a tactical advantage. Additionally, a meeting engagement may occur when one force attempts to deploy into a hasty defense while the other force attacks before its opponent can organize an effective defense. No matter how the force makes contact, seizing the initiative is the overriding imperative. Prompt execution of battle drills at platoon level and below, and standard actions on contact for larger units, can give that initiative to the friendly force.

MOVEMENT

2-64. In the context of Army tactics, **movement is the positioning of combat power to establish the conditions for maneuver**. To direct movement, Army forces use movement techniques, use movement formations, and conduct battle drills to mitigate the risk of making contact with the enemy before maneuvering. **Battle drills are rehearsed and well understood actions made in response to common battlefield occurrences**. They require a "go" order instead of a plan.

MUTUAL SUPPORT

2-65. *Mutual support* is that support which units render each other against an enemy, because of their assigned tasks, their position relative to each other and to the enemy, and their inherent capabilities (JP 3-31). In Army doctrine, mutual support is a planning consideration related to force disposition, not a command relationship. Commanders consider mutual support when task-organizing forces, assigning AOs, and positioning units. Mutual support has two aspects—supporting range and supporting distance.

2-66. Mutual support exists between two or more units or positions when they can support each other with direct or indirect fires, thus preventing an enemy from engaging one unit or position without being fired on from one or more adjacent units or positions. When a mutual support relationship exists between two or more units moving in relation to each other, those units can maneuver to obtain positional advantage over an enemy force engaging another unit. In the offense, a commander maneuvers subordinate forces to ensure some degree of mutual support between them.

2-67. In the defense, commanders select tactical positions to achieve the maximum degree of mutual support. Mutual support increases the strength of defensive positions, prevents an enemy force from attempting to defeat the defending friendly forces in detail, and helps prevent infiltration. When friendly forces are static, supporting range equals supporting distance.

OPERATION

2-68. An *operation* is a sequence of tactical actions with a common purpose and a unifying theme (JP 1). It includes the process of planning, preparing, executing, and assessing the offensive, defensive, and stability operations or defense support of civil authorities tasks and what may be needed to achieve the objectives of any engagement, battle, major operation, or campaign. It also includes enabling operations.

OPERATIONAL FRAMEWORK

2-69. An *operational framework* is a cognitive tool used to assist commanders and staffs in clearly visualizing and describing the application of combat power in time, space, purpose, and resources in the concept of operations (ADP 1-01). Army leaders are responsible for clearly articulating their visualization of operations in time, space, purpose, and resources. They do this through the Army operational framework and its associated vocabulary. (See ADP 3-0 for an additional discussion of the operational framework.)

2-70. The operational framework has four components. First, commanders are assigned an AO for the conduct of operations, from which, in turn, they assign AOs to subordinate units based on their visualization of an operation. Second, within their AO commanders may designate deep, close, support, and consolidation areas to describe the physical arrangement of forces in time, space, and purpose. Third, commanders establish decisive, shaping, and sustaining operations to further articulate an operation in terms of purpose. Finally, commanders designate main and supporting efforts to designate the shifting and prioritization of resources. (See ADP 3-0 for a discussion of the operational framework and deep, close, support, and consolidation areas.)

PIECEMEAL COMMITMENT

2-71. **Piecemeal commitment is the immediate employment of units in combat as they become available instead of waiting for larger aggregations of units to ensure mass, or the unsynchronized employment of available forces so that their combat power is not employed effectively**. Piecemeal commitment subjects the smaller committed forces to defeat in detail and prevents the massing and synchronizing of combat power with following maneuver and sustainment elements. However, piecemeal commitment may be advantageous to maintain momentum and to retain or exploit the initiative.

RECONSTITUTION

2-72. *Reconstitution* is those actions, including regeneration and reorganization, commanders plan and implement to restore units to a desired level of combat effectiveness commensurate with mission requirements and available resources (JP 3-02). Whereas reorganization is possible at the tactical level, regeneration requires support from higher echelons. Reconstitution is a total process and is not solely a sustainment operation. Commanders perform reconstitution when one or more subordinate units become combat ineffective, or when a commander can raise the combat effectiveness of a subordinate unit by shifting available resources. Reconstitution may include—
- Removing a unit from combat.
- Assessing a unit with external assets.
- Reestablishing a unit's chain of command.
- Training a unit for future operations.
- Reestablishing unit cohesion.

Reconstitution transcends the performance of normal day-to-day force sustainment tasks. However, it uses existing systems and units to do so. (See FM 4-95 for additional information on reconstitution.)

RESERVE

2-73. While joint doctrine has three definitions for reserve, the following Army definition applies to Army tactical operations. **A *reserve* is that portion of a body of troops that is withheld from action at the beginning of an engagement to be available for a decisive movement**. A reserve is an uncommitted force and thus does not normally have a full suite of combat multipliers available to it until it is committed. It is

Chapter 2

normally the echelon's main effort once it is committed. Commanders constitute a reserve and base the size of the reserve on the level of uncertainty in the current tactical situation. Commanders consider survivability and the most likely mission when positioning their reserve. While commanders can assign their reserve a wide variety of tasks to perform on commitment, a reserve remains prepared to accomplish other missions. The primary tasks for a reserve are to—

- Retain the initiative.
- Take advantage of unexpected success.
- Counter tactical reverses that threaten the integrity of the friendly force's operations.

A successful commander retains a reserve, reconstituting one whenever possible on the commitment of the original reserve.

RULES OF ENGAGEMENT

2-74. *Rules of engagement* are directives issued by competent military authority that delineate the circumstances and limitations under which United States forces will initiate and/or continue combat engagement with other forces encountered (JP 3-84). Operational requirements, policy, and law define the rules of engagement a commander must follow. Rules of engagement influence how a commander conducts operations by imposing political, practical, operational, and legal limitations. They may extend to criteria for initiating engagements with certain weapon systems, such as employing unobserved indirect fires within the echelon support and consolidation areas, or reacting to an attack. Unit commanders always retain the inherent right and obligation to exercise unit self-defense in response to a hostile act or demonstrated hostile intent. Unless otherwise directed by a unit commander, military members may exercise individual self-defense in response to a hostile act or demonstrated hostile intent. The Joint Chiefs of Staff have established standing rules of engagement. Operational-level commanders modify those standing rules of engagement as necessary. (See FM 1-04 for additional information on rules of engagement.)

SUPPORTING DISTANCE

2-75. *Supporting distance* is the distance between two units that can be traveled in time for one to come to the aid of the other and prevent its defeat by an enemy or ensure it regains control of a civil situation (ADP 3-0). For lower echelon units, it is the distance between two units that can be covered effectively by their fires. Supporting distance is a factor of combat power, dispositions, communications, and the tactical mobility of friendly and enemy forces.

SUPPORTING RANGE

2-76. *Supporting range* is the distance one unit may be geographically separated from a second unit yet remain within the maximum range of the second unit's weapons systems (ADP 3-0). Major factors that affect supporting range are terrain, the range of the supporting unit's weapon systems, and the locations of weapons systems in relation to a supported unit's position.

TACTICAL MOBILITY

2-77. **Tactical mobility is the ability of friendly forces to move and maneuver freely on the battlefield relative to the enemy**. Tactical mobility is a function of the relationship of cross-country mobility, firepower, and protection. The terrain, soil conditions, and weather affect cross-country mobility. Armored ground maneuver units, such as combined arms battalions, have good tactical mobility—except in restrictive terrain—combined with maximum firepower and protection. Infantry ground maneuver units, such as airborne infantry battalions, have a tactical mobility advantage against enemy armored forces in restrictive terrain, but they have limited firepower and protection. Stryker equipped forces also have good tactical mobility, but they possess less firepower and protection than armored forces. Army aviation maneuver units have excellent mobility in all but the most restrictive types of terrain, but they have limited protection. Extreme weather conditions also restrict the mobility of Army aviation units.

UNCOMMITTED FORCES

2-78. An *uncommitted force* is a force that is not in contact with an enemy and is not already deployed on a specific mission or course of action. Commanders use uncommitted forces to exploit success or avoid failure. Echelon reserves are examples of uncommitted forces.

WEIGHTING THE DECISIVE OPERATION OR MAIN EFFORT

2-79. The *decisive operation* is the operation that directly accomplishes the mission (ADP 3-0). Weighting the decisive operation or the main effort is a basic tactical concept closely associated with the mass and maneuver principles of war. The purpose for weighting the decisive operation or main effort is to concentrate the effects of combat power at the most advantageous place and time. A unit commander assumes risk in some areas to provide the resources required to mass combat power at a few key locations to support the unit's decisive operation or main effort.

FORMS OF MANEUVER AND FORMS OF THE DEFENSE

2-80. Leaders use the forms of maneuver and the forms of defense to elaborate COAs and schemes of maneuver. The forms describe the arrangement of friendly forces in relationship to the enemy. Understanding the simultaneity of decisive action is a key component of understanding the use of the forms of maneuver and defense. In operations where the preponderance of activities is offensive, there are units using a form of the defense. Similarly, in operations characterized by defensive activities, there are units using a form of maneuver. An example of this would be in a mobile defense where a static force conducts a defense of a linear obstacle while the striking force executes an envelopment.

2-81. *Forms of maneuver* **are distinct tactical combinations of fire and movement with a unique set of doctrinal characteristics that differ primarily in the relationship between the maneuvering force and the enemy**. The Army has five forms of maneuver—envelopment, frontal assault, infiltration, penetration, and turning movement. Combined arms organizations accomplish their missions by identifying when and where to execute these forms of maneuver. Commanders generally choose one form on which to build a COA. A higher echelon commander rarely specifies the specific form of maneuver a subordinate executes. However, that higher echelon commander's intent and guidance, along with the mission and any implied tasks, may impose constraints such as time, security, and direction of attack that narrow the forms of maneuver to one alternative. Additionally, the AO's characteristics and the enemy force's dispositions help commanders determine the form of maneuver. A single operation may contain several forms of maneuver. (See FM 3-90-1 for a discussion of these forms of maneuver.)

2-82. There are three forms of the defense—perimeter defense, defense of a linear obstacle, and reverse slope defense. Commanders address each form of the defense differently when planning and executing their defense. When required to expand on a type of defensive operation, they apply a form of defense.

ECHELONS

2-83. Army echelons have capabilities to perform different functions. These functions vary with the type of unit, the organization of the theater or joint operations area, the nature of the conflict, and the number and types of friendly forces committed to the effort. The echelons range from the fire team or crew, through the squad, section, platoon, company, battalion, and brigade to the division and corps.

2-84. At each echelon, a commander or leader task-organizes available capabilities to accomplish the mission. The purpose of task organization is to maximize different subordinate abilities to generate a combined arms effect consistent with the concept of operations. Commanders and staffs work to ensure the distribution of capabilities to the appropriate components of the force to weight the decisive operation and main effort. Command and support relationships describe the relationships between units within and supporting an echelon. (See ADP 5-0 for a discussion of these relationships.)

Chapter 2

FIRE TEAMS

2-85. **A *fire team* is a small military unit typically containing four or fewer Soldiers**. A fire team is usually grouped by two or three teams into a squad or section. The concept of the fire team is based on the need for tactical flexibility. A fire team is capable of autonomous operations as part of its next larger unit, such as a squad or section. It is usually led by a sergeant.

CREWS

2-86. **A *crew* is a small military unit that consists of all personnel operating a particular system**. This system might be a weapons system (such as a mortar or a machinegun). The system might also be a vehicle (such as a tank) or a sensor system (such as a target acquisition radar). Based on the system, the rank of the senior crewmember can vary widely from a junior noncommissioned officer to a commissioned or warrant officer.

SQUADS

2-87. **A *squad* is a small military unit typically containing two or more fire teams**. It typically contains a dozen Soldiers or less. In some cases, the crew of a system may also be designated as a squad. Squads are usually led by a staff sergeant.

SECTIONS

2-88. **A *section* is a tactical unit of the Army and Marine Corps smaller than a platoon and larger than a squad**. A section may consist of the crews of two or more Army systems, such as a tank section or several fire teams.

PLATOONS

2-89. **A *platoon* is a subdivision of a company or troop consisting of two or more squads or sections**. A platoon is normally led by a lieutenant. Platoons tend to contain roughly 30 Soldiers, but in some cases they contain significantly more or less than that number depending upon the type of formation.

COMPANIES, BATTERIES, TROOPS, AND DETACHMENTS

2-90. Companies, batteries, troops, and detachments are higher echelons than platoons. **A *company* is a unit consisting of two or more platoons, usually of the same type, with a headquarters and a limited capacity for self-support. A *troop* is a company-size unit in a cavalry organization. A *battery* is a company-size unit in a field artillery or air defense artillery battalion**. A company normally consists of more than 75 Soldiers. Some aviation and armor companies are exceptions to this rule. Companies and air defense and field artillery batteries are the basic elements of battalions. Companies, batteries, and troops may also be assigned as separate units to brigades and larger organizations. Some companies, such as special forces companies, have subordinate detachments instead of platoons, which are organized and trained to operate independently for extended periods. **A *detachment* is a tactical element organized on either a temporary or permanent basis for special duties**.

2-91. Company-size combat units can fight together or as subordinate platoons. Cavalry troops frequently operate with their platoons in separate areas. In combined arms battalions, companies either fight as organic units, or they are task-organized. **A *company team* is a combined arms organization formed by attaching one or more nonorganic armor, mechanized infantry, Stryker, or infantry platoons to an armor, mechanized infantry, Stryker, or infantry company, either in exchange for, or in addition to, its organic platoons**. These company teams can include other supporting squads or platoons, such as engineers. Company teams are task-organized for specific missions. Company teams can match capabilities to missions with greater precision than units using only organic platoons. However, the attachment of different units at the company level demands thorough training to achieve the maximum complementary effects. Whenever possible, platoons and detachments train together before their commitment to actual operations.

BATTALIONS AND SQUADRONS

2-92. **A *battalion* is a unit consisting of two or more company-, battery-, or troop-size units and a headquarters.** In cavalry organizations this echelon is called a squadron. Most battalions range in size from 500 to 800 Soldiers, although some sustainment battalions are larger. The Army organizes most of its battalions by branch, although most sustainment battalions contain a mix of functional organizations.

2-93. Maneuver battalions contain a headquarters company in addition to their branch-specific line companies. Combined arms battalions are exceptions to this rule in that they contain either two mechanized infantry companies and one armor company or one mechanized infantry company and two armor companies in addition to their headquarters company. Non-maneuver battalions typically have a headquarters detachment instead of a headquarters company. Typically, battalions have three to five companies in addition to their headquarters company.

2-94. A BCT commander can task-organize subordinate maneuver battalions with other maneuver and functional and multifunctional support companies to form task forces for special missions. **A *battalion task force* is a maneuver battalion-size unit consisting of a battalion headquarters, at least one assigned company-size element, and at least one attached company-size element from another maneuver or support unit (functional or multifunctional).** Task organization increases the capabilities of maneuver battalions. Field artillery battalions may control batteries of any kind from other field artillery battalions through an established support relationship. BCT commanders can reinforce engineer battalions with the same or different types of engineer companies and platoons to form engineer task forces.

2-95. Functional and multifunctional support and sustainment battalions vary widely in type and organization. They may perform functional services for a larger supported unit within that supported unit's AO. All types of battalions are capable of short-term, limited self-defense.

BRIGADES, REGIMENTS, AND GROUPS

2-96. Brigades, regiments, and groups are higher echelons than battalions. **A *brigade* is a unit consisting of two or more battalions and a headquarters company or detachment.** A brigade normally contains between 2,500 and 5,000 Soldiers. Its capacity for independent action varies by its type. Division commanders use armored, infantry, or Stryker BCTs, supported by multifunctional support brigades (including field artillery brigades, combat aviation brigades, maneuver enhancement brigades, and sustainment brigades) and functional brigades (including air and missile defense brigades, engineer brigades, civil affairs brigades, and military police brigades) to accomplish their missions. All types of brigades and BCTs can task-organize by the attachment or detachment of outside organizations to become brigade task forces.

2-97. **A *brigade combat team* is a combined arms organization consisting of a brigade headquarters, at least two maneuver battalions, and necessary supporting functional capabilities.** BCTs are the largest fixed tactical units in the Army. However, additional battalions and companies may be attached to them or their organic battalions, and companies can be detached from them. This occurs as part of force tailoring at the strategic and operational levels and as part of task organization at the tactical level. All types of BCTs—infantry, armored, and Stryker—normally contain a headquarters and headquarters company, a field artillery battalion, a brigade support battalion, a brigade engineer battalion, and a cavalry squadron. BCTs combine the efforts of their battalions and companies to fight engagements and perform tactical tasks within division-level battles and major operations. Their chief tactical responsibility is synchronizing the plans and actions of their subordinate units to accomplish tasks for a division headquarters. (See FM 3-96 for details on BCTs and their subordinate units.)

2-98. The Army currently retains only two tactical regiments, the 75th Ranger Regiment and the 160th Special Operations Aviation Regiment. All the Army's other regiments have no tactical function. Instead, they are intended to perpetuate regimental history, espirit de corps, and traditions for Soldiers affiliated with a regiment. Many of the Army's branches contain only a single regiment, such as the Corps of Engineers and the Military Police Corps. Each maneuver battalion or squadron carries an association with a parent regiment. In some BCTs and brigades several numbered battalions carrying the same regimental association serve together, and they tend to consider themselves part of the traditional regiment. In fact, they are independent battalions serving a brigade, rather than a regimental headquarters.

Chapter 2

2-99. Groups are brigade-size organizations that, because of Army modularity, are rarely used outside of Army's special operations forces. Army special operations forces use the term to designate large special forces and psychological operations units. The Army's modular design deactivated group headquarters in favor of activating additional brigade headquarters. Explosive ordnance disposal, criminal investigation division, regional support groups, specialized aviation units, and specialized intelligence units are exceptions to this rule.

DIVISIONS

2-100. **A *division* is an echelon of command and tactical formation that employs brigade combat teams, multi-functional brigades, and functional brigades to achieve objectives on land**. It is normally employed as a tactical headquarters that employs a combination of BCTs, multifunctional brigades, and functional brigades to operate as a formation. Two to five BCTs, a sustainment brigade, a combat aviation brigade, a division artillery headquarters and headquarters battery, and a maneuver enhancement brigade are assigned to a division conducting large-scale ground combat operations. A division headquarters is a self-contained organization with a command group and a fully functional staff that requires no staff support from subordinate units to provide capabilities for its primary role. The Army organizes each division headquarters staff into a division headquarters and headquarters battalion. That battalion is augmented by a reserve component main command post operational detachment to provide it with additional capacity. Functional support brigades consist of military police, engineer, air and missile defense, and military intelligence brigades. Functional support brigades normally have command relationships with a division headquarters (assigned, attached, operational control, or tactical control).

2-101. A division headquarters provides a flexible command and control capability in all operational environments. A division headquarters may be used in other roles, including acting as the senior Army headquarters, joint force land component, or a joint task force headquarters in a joint operations area for small-scale operations. However, when performing these roles, a division requires significant Army and joint augmentation.

2-102. The mission variables determine the optimal size and mix of capabilities of the forces task-organized under each division headquarters. The size, composition, and capabilities of the forces task-organized under a division headquarters may vary between divisions involved in the same joint campaign and may change from one phase of that campaign to another. Operations focused on the destruction of a conventional enemy may require a mix of forces and capabilities that differ from those required for an operation focused on protection of civil populations.

2-103. A division normally operates as a tactical headquarters under the operational control of an Army corps, ARFOR, or joint force land component commander. The *ARFOR* is the Army component and senior Army headquarters of all Army forces assigned or attached to a combatant command, subordinate joint force command, joint functional command, or multinational command (FM 3-94). As a tactical echelon, a division headquarters arranges multiple tactical actions of its subordinates in time, space, and purpose to achieve significant military objectives. A division headquarters leverages joint force capabilities and conducts shaping operations within its AO to create favorable conditions for the success of its subordinate units. A division headquarters allocates resources, designates the main and supporting efforts, forecasts operational requirements, and establishes the priorities of support within its task-organized forces. Sustainment, medical, and functional units (including military police, engineer, air and missile defense, and military intelligence) in command or support relationships with a division operate in accordance with established priorities.

CORPS

2-104. A *corps* is an echelon of command and tactical formation that employs divisions, multi-functional brigades, and functional brigades to achieve objectives on land. Large-scale combat operations may require a corps headquarters to function as a tactical land headquarters under an operational-level command, such as a joint or multinational land component command. A corps headquarters is organized, trained, and equipped to control the operations of two to five divisions, together with supporting theater-level organizations. The distinguishing differences between corps and division operations are their scope and scale. During large-scale combat operations, a corps conducting tactical operations operates as a large combined arms formation employing capabilities within and across multiple domains, not just as a headquarters. Normally, a corps exercises operational control over two or more Army divisions and a variety of multifunctional and functional supporting brigades. It exercises tactical control over various Marine Corps units and multinational units, and it is supported by various theater military intelligence, signal, and sustainment organizations and joint combat support agencies. The corps has both operational and administrative responsibilities.

2-105. A corps receives capabilities and units from the theater army to conduct operations. There is no standard organizational structure for a corps. However, a corps generally requires a maneuver enhancement brigade, a combat aviation brigade, an expeditionary sustainment command, a field artillery brigade, and a theater military intelligence brigade to conduct large-scale combat operations. Other units may provide direct or general support.

2-106. Based on the tasks of the divisions and the allocation of brigades, the corps commander determines the appropriate command and support relationships for subordinate divisions and brigades. A corps may retain a division or some number of brigades in reserve or for consolidation of gains activities. (However, an exception to this is that field artillery brigades are not retained in reserve or used for consolidation of gains activities.)

FIELD ARMIES

2-107. **A *field army* is an echelon of command that employs multiple corps, divisions, multi-functional brigades, and functional brigades to achieve objectives on land.** The field army is the only echelon above the brigade that is only a headquarters. Large-scale combat operations involving multiple corps may require the establishment of a field army to function as the senior tactical or operational-level command exercising command and control over multiple corps-sized formations. The field army's primary role is to serve as the ARFOR or joint force land component command for multi-corps operations. When serving as the joint force land component command, field armies require significant augmentation from the joint and multinational force. They are most likely to be employed in theaters where peer and near-peer adversaries have the capability of conducting large-scale ground combat. Field armies possess no standardized force structure. The Army tailors each field army to the conditions prevailing in its assigned area of responsibility. The field army receives the necessary capabilities and units from external sources based on its requirements.

This page intentionally left blank.

Chapter 3

The Offense

This chapter discusses the basics of the offense. These basics include the purposes of the offense, characteristics of the offense, types of offensive operations, common offensive control measures, common offensive planning considerations, and transitions. These basics apply to all types of offensive operations.

PURPOSES OF THE OFFENSE

3-1. The offense is the decisive form of war. The offense is the ultimate means commanders have of imposing their will on enemy forces. Army forces conduct the offense to defeat and destroy enemy forces as well as gain control of terrain, resources, and population centers. Commanders may also conduct the offense to deceive or divert an enemy force, develop intelligence, or hold an enemy force in position. Commanders seize, retain, and exploit the initiative when conducting the offense. Specific operations may orient on an enemy force or terrain objective to achieve a position of relative advantage. Taking the initiative from an enemy force requires the conduct of the offense, even in the defense.

3-2. The main purposes of the offense are to defeat enemy forces, destroy enemy forces, and gain control of terrain, resources, and population centers. Additionally, commanders conduct the offense to—
- Secure decisive terrain.
- Deprive the enemy of resources.
- Gain information.
- Deceive and divert an enemy force.
- Fix an enemy force in position.
- Disrupt an enemy force's attack.
- Set the conditions for successful future operations.

The offense supports friendly operations in the air, maritime, space, and cyberspace domains, and in the information environment. These operations destroy, dislocate, disintegrate, or isolate an enemy force.

CHARACTERISTICS OF THE OFFENSE

3-3. Audacity, concentration, surprise, and tempo characterize the offense. Commanders maneuver forces to advantageous positions before an operation. To shape their decisive operation, they initiate selective contact with enemy forces. The decisive operation determines the outcome of the major operation, battle, or engagement. Decisive operations capitalize on the successful application of the characteristics of the offense. (See paragraph 2-79 for more on decisive operations.)

AUDACITY

3-4. Audacity is a willingness to take bold risks. The offense favors the bold execution of plans. Commanders display audacity by accepting risks commensurate with the value of their objectives. Commanders dispel uncertainty by acting decisively. They compensate for any lack of information by developing the situation aggressively to seize the initiative, and then they continuously engage in combat to exploit opportunities as they arise.

Chapter 3

CONCENTRATION

3-5. Concentration is massing the effects of combat power in time and space at the decisive point to achieve a single purpose. Concentration requires the coordination of unified action partner capabilities in multiple domains to create opportunities that enable offensive land operations. Information systems provide relevant information that helps commanders determine when to concentrate their forces. By massing combat power rapidly along converging axes and synchronizing the effects of supporting assets in multiple domains, attackers overwhelm enemy forces. Commanders adopt the tactics for the situation, protect the force, and sustain the attack's tempo.

3-6. To protect their forces before they concentrate, commanders apply joint assets to prevent enemy detection and interdiction. They request ground, air, maritime, space, and cyberspace resources to delay, disrupt, or destroy enemy reconnaissance capabilities. Commanders may keep their forces concentrated after a successful attack to take advantage of their momentum or disperse them to avoid becoming vulnerable to enemy counteraction.

SURPRISE

3-7. Commanders surprise enemy forces by attacking at a time or place or in a manner for which enemy forces did not prepare or expect. Commanders achieve surprise by showing enemy forces what they expect to see while actually doing something different. Surprise delays enemy reactions, overloads and confuses enemy command and control systems, induces psychological shock, and reduces the coherence of an enemy force's defense. Correct assessment of an enemy commander's intent and a clear sense of timing are necessary to achieve surprise.

3-8. Operational and tactical surprise complement each other. Operational surprise creates the conditions for successful tactical operations. Tactical surprise can cause an enemy force to hesitate or misjudge a situation, creating operational opportunities. Effective commanders exploit surprise before an enemy force realizes what is happening and can effectively react.

3-9. Modern surveillance and warning systems, the availability of commercial space-based imagery products, and global commercial news and social networks make surprise more difficult to achieve than in the past. Commanders deceive an enemy force as to the nature, timing, and objective of an attack by using bad weather, seemingly impassable terrain, and military deception to shape enemy perceptions. Airborne, air assault, and special operations forces attacks—combined with strikes by Army and joint fires against objectives an enemy force regards as secure—create disruptive or debilitating cognitive effects on enemy soldiers and commanders. The VII and XVIII Corps' turning movement into the flank and rear of the Iraqi Republican Guard during OPERATION DESERT STORM is a historical example of achieving operational surprise during the offense.

TEMPO

3-10. *Tempo* is the relative speed and rhythm of military operations over time with respect to the enemy (ADP 3-0). Controlling tempo is necessary to retain the initiative. An attack that achieves results more quickly than enemy forces can respond disrupts enemy plans. Maintaining a high tempo requires initiative on the part of subordinates within their commander's intent. Mission orders allow subordinates the flexibility to react swiftly to opportunities and threats and maintain a high tempo.

3-11. Commanders adjust tempo continuously. The flexibility of any tactical situation, sustainment realities, or enemy actions affect tempo. Rapid tempo demands quick decisions informed by accurate running estimates. Maintaining rapid tempo continually creates opportunities and reduces friendly vulnerabilities. Maintaining rapid tempo also denies enemy forces the chance to rest or synchronize the employment of their combat power.

3-12. By increasing tempo, commanders maintain momentum. They plan for rapid transitions and ensure sustainment operations do not prevent premature culmination of the offense. Attackers shift combat power quickly to widen penetrations, exploit exposed flanks, and reinforce successes. Friendly forces attack in depth with fires and maneuver to destroy or disrupt an enemy commander's ability to command and control enemy forces. Commanders never permit enemy forces to recover from the shock of an initial assault. They prevent defenders from massing effects against the friendly decisive operation.

TYPES OF OFFENSIVE OPERATIONS

3-13. The four types of offensive operations are movement to contact, attack, exploitation, and pursuit. The types of offensive operations describe friendly force arrangements by purpose.

MOVEMENT TO CONTACT

3-14. *Movement to contact* **is a type of offensive operation designed to develop the situation and to establish or regain contact**. The goal of a movement to contact is to make initial contact with a small element while retaining enough combat power to develop the situation and mitigate the associated risk. A movement to contact creates favorable conditions for subsequent tactical actions. Commanders conduct a movement to contact when an enemy situation is vague or not specific enough to conduct an attack. A movement to contact may result in a meeting engagement. Meeting engagements are combat actions that occur when an incompletely deployed force engages an enemy at an unexpected time and place. Once an enemy force makes contact, the commander has five options: attack, defend, bypass, delay, or withdraw. Subordinate variations of a movement to contact include search and attack and cordon and search operations.

ATTACK

3-15. **An *attack* is a type of offensive operation that destroys or defeats enemy forces, seizes and secures terrain, or both**. Attacks incorporate coordinated movement supported by fires. They may be part of either decisive or shaping operations. A commander may describe an attack as hasty or deliberate, depending on the time available for assessing the situation, planning, and preparing. A commander may decide to conduct an attack using only fires, based on an analysis of the mission variables. An attack differs from a movement to contact because in an attack commanders know at least part of an enemy's dispositions. This knowledge enables commanders to better synchronize and employ combat power.

3-16. Variations of the attack are ambush, counterattack, demonstration, feint, raid, and spoiling attack. The commander's intent and the mission variables guide which of these variations of attack to employ. Commanders conduct each of these variations, except for a raid, as either a hasty or a deliberate operation.

EXPLOITATION

3-17. **An *exploitation* is a type of offensive operation that usually follows a successful attack and is designed to disorganize the enemy in depth**. Exploitations seek to disintegrate enemy forces to the point where they have no alternative but to surrender or retreat. Exploitations take advantage of tactical opportunities. Division and higher echelon headquarters normally plan exploitations as branches or sequels.

PURSUIT

3-18. **A *pursuit* is a type of offensive operation designed to catch or cut off a hostile force attempting to escape, with the aim of destroying it**. There are two variations of the pursuit: frontal and combination. A pursuit normally follows a successful exploitation. However, if enemy resistance breaks down and enemy forces begin fleeing the battlefield, any type of offensive operation can transition into a pursuit. Pursuits entail rapid movement and decentralized control. Bold action and calculated initiative are required in the conduct of a pursuit. The Third U.S. Army's actions in France between August and September 1944 during World War II is an example of a pursuit.

COMMON OFFENSIVE CONTROL MEASURES

3-19. Commanders use common offensive control measures to synchronize the effects of combat power. Chapter 2 introduced airspace coordinating measures, permissive FSCMs, and restrictive FSCMs used in the offense. Commanders use the minimum control measures required to synchronize the application of the combat power required to accomplish their mission. This provides subordinates the flexibility needed to

Chapter 3

respond to changes in the situation. Understanding and using commonly understood control measures enable commanders and staffs to develop and publish clear and concise mission orders, as well as direct tactical actions quickly, with minimal communication during execution.

ASSAULT POSITION

3-20. An *assault position* is a covered and concealed position short of the objective from which final preparations are made to assault the objective. Final preparations include short halts to coordinate the final assault, reorganizing to adjust to combat losses or to adjust the attacking force's dispositions. Final preparations can also involve technical activities, such as engineers performing their final prepare-to-fire checks on obstacle clearing systems and the crews of plow- or roller-equipped tanks removing their locking pins. An assault position may be located near a final coordination line or a probable line of deployment.

ASSAULT TIME

3-21. **The *assault time* is the moment to attack the initial objectives throughout the geographical scope of the operation.** A higher echelon headquarters imposes this time during the offense to achieve simultaneous results. It is similar to the time on target control method for fire mission processing used by the field artillery. A commander uses it instead of a time of attack because of the different distances that different elements of the force must traverse, known obstacles, and differences in unit tactical mobility.

ATTACK BY FIRE POSITION

3-22. **An *attack by fire position* is the general position from which a unit performs the tactical task of attack by fire.** The purpose of these positions is to mass the effects of direct fire systems from one or multiple locations on the enemy. An attack by fire position does not indicate the specific site. An attack by fire position normally applies to company-size and smaller units.

ATTACK POSITION

3-23. **The *attack position* is the last position an attacking force occupies or passes through before crossing the line of departure.** An attack position facilitates the deployment and last minute coordination of an attacking force before it crosses the line of departure (LD). (See paragraph 3-31 for a discussion of the LD.) It is located on the friendly side of the LD and offers cover and concealment. Whenever possible, units move through their attack positions without stopping. If a unit occupies an attack position, it stays there for the shortest amount of time possible to avoid offering the enemy a target.

AXIS OF ADVANCE

3-24. **An *axis of advance* is the general area through which the bulk of a unit's combat power must move.** When developing an axis of advance, a commander also establishes bypass criteria. ***Bypass criteria* are measures established by higher echelon headquarters that specify the conditions and size under which enemy units and contact may be avoided.** A commander uses an axis of advance—

- First, to direct the bypass of locations that could delay the progress of an advancing force, such as known contaminated areas.
- Second, to indicate that a force is not required to clear the AO as it advances. The force will need to clear the axis in accordance with specified bypass criteria.
- Third, to indicate to a unit involved in offensive encirclement, exploitation, or pursuit operations the need to move rapidly toward an objective.

BATTLE HANDOVER LINE

3-25. **The *battle handover line* is a designated phase line where responsibility transitions from the stationary force to the moving force and vice versa.** The common higher echelon commander of two forces establishes a battle handover line after consulting both commanders. The stationary commander determines the location of the line. The battle handover line is forward of the forward edge of the battle area (FEBA) in the defense or the forward line of own troops (FLOT) in the offense. The commander draws it to keep the passing unit in the supporting range of the forward combat elements of the stationary unit until the passage of lines is complete. The area between the battle handover line and the stationary force belongs to the stationary force commander. The stationary force commander may employ security forces, obstacles, and fires in the area.

DIRECTION OF ATTACK

3-26. **The *direction of attack* is a specific direction or assigned route a force uses and does not deviate from when attacking**. It is a restrictive control measure. A commander's use of a direction of attack maximizes control over a subordinate unit's movement, and it is often used during night attacks, infiltrations, and when attacking through obscurants. Unit commanders establish a direction of attack through a variety of means, such as target reference points and checkpoints. When using a direction of attack, unit commanders designate a point of departure. (See paragraph 3-33 for a discussion of the point of departure.)

FINAL COORDINATION LINE

3-27. **The *final coordination line* is a phase line close to the enemy position used to coordinate the lifting or shifting of supporting fires with the final deployment of maneuver elements**. Before crossing this line, units make final adjustments to supporting fires to reflect the actual situation versus the anticipated situation. The location should be easily recognizable on the ground. The final coordination line is not an FSCM.

FORWARD LINE OF OWN TROOPS

3-28. The *forward line of own troops* is a line which indicates the most forward positions of friendly forces in any kind of military operation at a specific time (JP 3-03). The FLOT normally identifies the forward location of covering or screening forces. In the defense, it may be beyond, at, or short of the FEBA. It does not apply to small, long-range reconnaissance assets and similar stay-behind forces. Friendly forces forward of the FLOT may have a restrictive FSCM, such as a restrictive fire area, placed around them to prevent friendly fire incidents.

LIMIT OF ADVANCE

3-29. **The *limit of advance* is a phase line used to control forward progress of the attack**. The attacking unit does not advance any of its elements or assets beyond the LOA, but the attacking unit can push its security forces to that limit. Commanders usually select a feature that is easily identifiable, perpendicular to the direction of attack, and on the far side of the objective as the LOA. The use of an LOA prevents an attacking force from overextending and reduces fratricide possibilities and friendly fire incidents by fires supporting the attack. Unit commanders position an LOA far enough beyond an objective to allow their unit to flexibly defend it. An LOA prevents units from exploiting success and launching a pursuit. Commanders should only use LOAs if they do not want their units to conduct an exploitation or pursuit. An LOA and the unit's forward boundary should rarely coincide because of limitations that a forward boundary places on supporting fires beyond that boundary.

LINE OF CONTACT

3-30. **The *line of contact* is a general trace delineating the location where friendly and enemy forces are engaged**. Commanders designate the enemy side of the line of contact by the abbreviation "ENY." In the defense, a line of contact is often synonymous with the FLOT. A line of contact may be combined with an LD in the offense.

LINE OF DEPARTURE

3-31. In land warfare, the *line of departure* is a line designated to coordinate the departure of attack elements (JP 3-31). The purpose of an LD is to coordinate the advance of the attacking force, so that its elements strike enemy forces in the order and at the time desired. An LD also marks where a unit transitions from movement to maneuver. Commanders also use it to facilitate the coordination of fires. Generally, it should be perpendicular to the direction the attacking force takes on its way to the objective. Units have different movement rates based on their mobility characteristics and the terrain surrounding their assembly areas. Commanders consider these different characteristics when establishing an LD to prevent these differences from affecting synchronization. When possible, commanders select an LD that provides cover for the unit's deployment into a combat formation before crossing the LD. In many cases, an LD is also a line of contact because the unit in contact is conducting the attack from its current positions.

OBJECTIVE

3-32. **An *objective* is a location used to orient operations, phase operations, facilitate changes of direction, and provide for unity of effort.** An objective can be terrain or force oriented. Terrain-oriented objectives should be easy to recognize. A higher echelon commander uses terrain-oriented objectives to focus the operations of subordinates, focus phase operations, facilitate changes of direction, and provide for unity of effort. Commanders determine force-oriented objectives based on known enemy positions. Commanders may assign intermediate objectives as necessary; however, they generally only assign subordinate commanders their final objectives.

POINT OF DEPARTURE

3-33. **The *point of departure* is the point where the unit crosses the line of departure and begins moving along a direction of attack.** Units conducting patrols and other operations in a low-visibility environment commonly use a point of departure as a control measure. Like an LD, it marks the point where the unit transitions from movement to maneuver under conditions of limited visibility.

PROBABLE LINE OF DEPLOYMENT

3-34. **A *probable line of deployment* is a phase line that designates the location where the commander intends to deploy the unit into assault formation before beginning the assault.** Units, primarily at battalion echelons and below, use a probable line of deployment when they intend to cross an LD when they are not in their assault formations. It is usually a linear terrain feature perpendicular to the direction of attack and recognizable under conditions of limited visibility. Units ideally locate the probable line of deployment outside the range that enemy forces can place the attacking force under effective direct fire.

RALLY POINT

3-35. A *rally point* is an easily identifiable point on the ground at which units can reassemble and reorganize if they become dispersed (ATP 3-21.20). Forces conducting a patrol or an infiltration commonly use this control measure. **The *objective rally point* is an easily identifiable point where all elements of the infiltrating unit assemble and prepare to attack the objective.** It is typically near the infiltrating unit's objective; however, there is no standard distance from the objective to the objective rally point. It should be far enough away from the objective so that enemy forces will not detect the infiltrating unit's attack preparations.

SUPPORT BY FIRE POSITION

3-36. **A *support by fire position* is the general position from which a unit performs the tactical mission task of support by fire.** The purpose of a support by fire position is to increase the supported force's freedom of maneuver by placing direct fires on an objective that a friendly force assaults. Commanders select support by fire positions so that the moving assault force does not mask its supporting fires. Support by fire positions are normally located on the flank of the assault force and elevated above the objective. Support by fire positions rarely apply to units larger than company size.

TARGET CONTROL MEASURES

3-37. A target is an area designated and numbered for future firing. Target graphic control measures are different for point targets, linear targets, and area targets. To support a maneuver phase, individual point or single targets can combine into a target series or target groups. A group of targets consists of two or more targets on which a force may place simultaneous fires. A series of targets is fired in a predetermined time sequence once the series is initiated. Commanders use target series and target groups in various combinations as required. (A target can also be a person, place, or thing, such as a tank or a group of people against which messages are directed.) Target control measures also apply in the defense.

TIME OF ATTACK

3-38. **The *time of attack* is the moment the leading elements of the main body cross the line of departure, or in a limited-visibility attack, the point of departure**. A commander uses it when conducting simultaneous operations where a shaping operation must accomplish its mission to create the conditions for success of the decisive operation. When determining the time of attack, commanders consider the time subordinates require to—

- Conduct necessary reconnaissance, prepare plans, and issue orders.
- Synchronize plans between all subordinate units.
- Complete attack preparations, such as pre-combat checks and inspections.
- Move to an LD or a point of departure.

Commanders designate the time of attack in orders. This is generally when the main body crosses an LD. However, the headquarters planning the offense specifies the term's exact meaning.

COMMON OFFENSIVE PLANNING CONSIDERATIONS

3-39. Commanders understand, visualize, describe, and direct. They understand their AO, their mission, and the capabilities of their forces. Commanders create shared understanding by developing and issuing planning guidance based on their visualization of how to solve tactical problems. They then direct COA development and execution of the plan.

3-40. An attacking force's principal advantage is the initiative. Having the initiative allows commanders to select the time, place, and methods used by attacking forces. An attacking commander has the opportunity to develop a plan and concentrate the capabilities of subordinate forces in a specific manner, time, and location that is most disadvantageous to an enemy force. Commanders focus on attacking the right combination of targets to accomplish the mission at the least cost. They create exploitable opportunities through rapid, violently executed, and unpredictable attacks that minimize an enemy force's ability to respond.

3-41. Each battle or engagement has unique characteristics, such as the types of weapons, degree of tactical mobility, and the influence of various capabilities across multiple domains. The commanders most likely to enjoy tactical success are those able to visualize the battlefield, understand the implications of existing friendly and enemy dispositions, and take effective action first. Commanders maintain this momentum by following up attacks quickly to deny enemy forces any opportunity to adjust or adapt to the new situation. The tempo of friendly operations must be fast enough to prevent effective enemy counteraction. Commanders maintain pressure by adjusting combinations of friendly capabilities to exploit initial gains and create further dilemmas for an enemy commander.

COMMAND AND CONTROL

3-42. Commanders, assisted by their staffs, integrate numerous processes and activities within their headquarters and across the force as they exercise command and control. A commander's intent and mission, in the context of the mission variables, determine the concept of operations. The concept of operations expands on the commander's intent by describing how the commander wants the force to accomplish the mission. It states the principal tasks required, the responsible subordinate units, and the ways principal tasks complement one another. (See ADP 6-0 for a discussion of command and control.)

Operations Process

3-43. Commanders assign missions commensurate with the capabilities of the units in their task organization. The commander's role in the operations process is to understand, visualize, describe, direct, lead, and assess the performance of tasks by their units.

3-44. All offensive planning addresses the mission variables. During offensive planning, commanders and staffs place special emphasis on—
- Missions and objectives, including task and purpose, for each subordinate element.
- Commander's intent.
- Enemy positions, obstacles, strengths, and capabilities.
- AOs for the use of each subordinate element with associated control graphics.
- Time the operation is to begin.
- Scheme of maneuver.
- Targeting guidance and high-payoff targets.
- Special tasks required to accomplish the mission.
- Communicating risk.
- Options for accomplishing the mission.
- Transition to stability operations once large scale combat ceases.

3-45. Planning efforts must address the requirement for corps and divisions to conduct operations in their deep areas to create conditions that allow subordinate BCTs to conduct successful combat operations in the close area. BCTs and divisions assigned to consolidation areas likewise require planning support for those aspects for which they have few organic capabilities, such as civil affairs.

3-46. Commanders and staffs translate a unit's mission into specific objectives for all subordinates. (Reserve forces have planning priorities, not objectives.) These objectives can involve the conduct of the offense. If the assigned type of offensive operation has associated forms of maneuver, a commander may specify which form to use, but effective commanders minimize actions that restrict subordinates' freedom of action. (See ADP 5-0 for a discussion of the military decision-making process.)

3-47. Commanders guide the actions of subordinates during execution. Based on their visualization of the operation, commanders position themselves where they can best influence critical events and make critical decisions, such as changing priorities of support or employing reserves. This normally means that commanders are well forward, usually with the force conducting the decisive operation or designated as the main effort. Once the decisive operation or main effort makes contact with enemy forces, the commander assesses the situation and directs appropriate action as necessary.

3-48. Commanders consider how to exploit advantages that arise during the execution of the offense. They anticipate requirements to shift the decisive operation or main effort during the offense to press an engagement and keep enemy forces off balance. They develop decision points to support these changes and use both human and technical means to validate the timing of these decisions.

3-49. Commanders consider the presence of civilians within their AOs on their operations and determine what minimum-essential stability tasks their units need to perform. All units have the capability to perform stability tasks if the tactical situation allows. These minimum-essential stability tasks generally involve some aspects of civil control, civil security, and the restoration of essential services.

3-50. Units conduct offensive operations until they defeat the enemy forces in their AOs. Once major combat operations cease, units may transition to consolidate gains. Commanders clearly articulate to their subordinates this transition by changing the rules of engagement and allocating combat power complementary to the shift in the operational environment from one characterized principally by offensive and defensive operations, to another with greater emphasis on stability tasks.

3-51. Following the conclusion of large-scale combat in an AO, units perform security first and then progress to stability-related tasks. Units first address the final defeat of all enemy means of resistance and secure key terrain, infrastructure, and populations. Only then do units consider stability tasks above the minimum required by the law of war. Planning to consolidate gains is primarily a corps and division responsibility that occurs before, during, and after large-scale ground combat and includes allocating resources to consolidate gains. When the shift to stability operations occurs, the staff disseminates the change in purpose down to the lowest echelons.

Team Development Between Commanders

3-52. Commanders rely on others to execute their intent. Turning intent into reality takes the combined efforts of teams from both inside and outside their organizations. Commanders build effective teams through professional development and training. During combat, they organize their forces to accomplish their missions based on their concept of operations. They assign responsibilities, establish or delegate appropriate command or support relationships, and establish coordinating instructions. Sound organization provides for unity of effort, centralized planning, and decentralized execution. Unity of effort is necessary for effectiveness and efficiency. Centralized planning is essential for controlling and coordinating the efforts of friendly forces. Simplicity and clarity are critical when organizing Army forces with multinational forces and other unified action partners.

Degraded Communications

3-53. All units conducting offensive operations should expect to operate in a contested and degraded communications environment. Degradation may arise from environmental circumstances, enemy action directed against friendly communications and information systems, or malfunctions. A degraded communications environment may be permanent or temporary. The use of mission orders and commander's intent is critical to remaining effective in a degraded communications environment, regardless of the source of the degradation. (See FM 6-02 for more information on how units receive signal support.)

3-54. Enemies use several methods to deny friendly use of the cyberspace domain and the electromagnetic spectrum. These methods include cyberspace attack (digital attack against Army, joint, and other networks), electronic attack (jamming of portions of the electromagnetic spectrum), and physical attack against infrastructure and electronics. Units at each echelon require standard operating procedures and drills for restoring functionality and connectivity.

3-55. A unit can employ any number of measures to restore functionality to degraded communications and information systems. A unit may—
- Use printed maps and overlays to maintain a common operational picture within a command post.
- Use combat network radios to transmit orders and reports.
- Increase the use of liaison officers.
- Use couriers to transport orders, reports, and other information between headquarters and between maneuver units, using written orders, overlays, or digital media.
- Run fiber-optic and telephone cables between headquarters. (Commanders and staffs should be aware that this technique increases the time required to establish and displace command posts.)
- Displace to terrain that protects headquarters from enemy jamming.
- Limit electronic emissions.

Lower echelon units have the responsibility to restore communications with their higher echelon. Each impacted element restores communications using available resources and does not rely on protocols for establishing communications and liaison (from higher to lower, left to right, supporting to supported) to govern efforts to restore those communications. Units establish maximum time lapse interval standards for contact to be reestablished and the methods used to reestablish them. Commanders normally direct this as part of the operation order through a detailed primary, alternate, contingency, and emergency communication (PACE) plan.

MOVEMENT AND MANEUVER

3-56. Commanders seek to create multiple dilemmas to prevent an enemy force from reacting in an organized fashion. They achieve this by moving forces to positions that compel enemy decisions that favor the friendly commander. When required, security forces prevent an enemy force from discerning friendly dispositions, capabilities, and intentions, or interfering with the preparations for the attack.

3-57. *Close combat* is warfare carried out on land in a direct-fire fight, supported by direct and indirect fires and other assets (ADP 3-0). Close combat encompasses all actions that place friendly forces in immediate contact with an enemy force where commanders use direct fire and movement in combination to defeat or destroy enemy forces or gain control and retain ground, often through shock effect. Shock effect describes a temporary partial mental paralysis that an individual or a unit can experience after a sudden upsetting or surprising event and that prevents an immediate effective response to that event.

3-58. Seizing or retaining terrain that provides advantages to friendly force maneuver allows commanders to gain and maintain positions of relative advantage. For military purposes, terrain includes physical (geographic) and non-physical (virtual and cognitive) components. Commanders and staffs include the cognitive and virtual considerations of an operational environment when describing terrain. Terrain that is of importance to commanders is described as key or decisive terrain. **Key terrain is an identifiable characteristic whose seizure or retention affords a marked advantage to either combatant.** *Decisive terrain* **is key terrain whose seizure and retention is mandatory for successful mission accomplishment**. If decisive terrain is present, commanders designate it to communicate its importance in the commander's concept of operations, first to the echelon staff and later to subordinate commanders.

Armored and Stryker Forces

3-59. Armored and Stryker units provide inherent mobility capabilities. Armored units provide firepower and protection at the cost of heavy sustainment requirements and limitations in restrictive terrain. Stryker units provide firepower and great mobility out of contact, but they lack protection against many anti-armor systems. Both types can operate in CBRN contaminated environments because of their built-in collective CBRN protection systems. Each has capabilities that, when applied correctly, place a defending enemy force in a position of disadvantage. Armored and Stryker units can employ any of the forms of maneuver that are situationally appropriate, although the use of the envelopment tends to provide the greatest payoff. Armored units are particularly effective when conducting mobile combat against enemy forces in open terrain. Stryker units use terrain to maneuver outside of direct fire range and then employ their infantry to close with the enemy. The combat vehicles in these forces allow commanders to rapidly maneuver subordinate forces to positions of advantage against defending enemy forces and then immediately move to other locations to disrupt the integrity of an enemy's defense.

Dismounted Infantry Forces

3-60. Dismounted infantry forces are best suited for the offense in complex terrain. Dismounted infantry forces employ any forms of maneuver to secure objectives and achieve exploitable positions of advantage over an enemy force. Those positions of advantage may allow follow-on armored and Stryker forces to exploit that success, or they may block enemy counterattacking forces. Dismounted infantry forces can conduct air assaults, providing a division commander with a rapidly deployable force. Any application of dismounted infantry requires considerations for protection and supporting systems.

Rotary-Wing Aviation and Unmanned Aircraft Systems

3-61. Army aviation units conduct air-ground operations as the aviation maneuver force of the combined arms team. Army aviation units increase the combat power, agility, flexibility, and survivability of the entire combined arms team.

3-62. During offensive operations, aviation units and systems normally integrate into the scheme of maneuver and are given missions similar to those of ground maneuver units. Aviation forces conduct attacks, air assaults, and reconnaissance. They can deploy aerial minefields and conduct security operations. Attack helicopters are most effective in conditions of limited visibility against exposed enemy forces on the move. They are less effective against enemy forces in prepared defensive positions.

3-63. Unmanned aircraft systems conduct reconnaissance, surveillance, and information collection in areas where there may be excessive risk to manned aircraft. Commanders can employ some types of unmanned aircraft systems as attack assets. These systems work effectively with manned aircraft and when supporting indirect fires to increase the depth and breadth of aviation reconnaissance and maneuver. The longer unmanned systems loiter over a reconnaissance objective, the greater their ability to gain and maintain enemy contact. (See FM 3-04 for additional information on the employment of Army aviation in the offense.)

Movement Formations

3-64. A *movement formation* **is an ordered arrangement of forces for a specific purpose and describes the general configuration of a unit on the ground.** Commanders can use seven different movement formations depending on the mission variables: column, line, echelon (left or right), box, diamond, wedge, and vee. Terrain characteristics and visibility determine the actual arrangement and location of the unit's personnel and vehicles within a given formation. (FM 3-90-1 describes these combat formations.)

3-65. Movement formations allow a unit to move on a battlefield in a posture suited to the commander's intent and mission. A unit may employ a series of movement formations during the course of an attack; each has its advantages and disadvantages. Subordinate units within a movement formation can also employ their own movement formations, consistent with their particular situation. To determine the appropriate formation, commanders consider the advantages and disadvantages of each formation in the areas of command, control, maintenance, firepower orientation, ability to mass fires, and flexibility. All movement formations use one or more of the three movement techniques: traveling, traveling overwatch, and bounding overwatch. (See FM 3-90-1 for a description of the movement techniques.)

3-66. The use of standard formations allows units to shift from one formation to another, giving additional flexibility when adjusting to changes in the tactical situation and terrain. By designating the movement formation planned for use, commanders—

- Establish the geographic relationship between units.
- Indicate probable reactions once an enemy makes contact with the formation.
- Indicate the level of security desired.
- Establish the primary orientation of subordinate weapon systems.
- Posture friendly forces for the attack.

The number of subordinate maneuver units available to a headquarters may make some movement formations impractical.

Soldiers' Load

3-67. The load that Soldiers carry is an important planning consideration. How much Soldiers carry, how far, and in what configuration are critical mission considerations requiring command emphasis and inspection. Historical experience and research show that Soldiers can carry 30 percent of their body weight and retain much of their agility, stamina, alertness, and mobility. At times conditions dictate that a Soldier's load must exceed this recommended weight. Effective commanders and subordinate leaders account for how excess weight influences the effectiveness of their units and adjust planning accordingly.

ASSURED MOBILITY

3-68. *Assured mobility* is a framework—of processes, actions, and capabilities—that assures the ability of a force to deploy, move, and maneuver where and when desired, to achieve the commander's intent (ATP 3-90.4). The assured mobility fundamentals of prediction, detection, prevention, avoidance, neutralization, and protection support framing staff planning of subordinate unit tasks and activities. The assured mobility framework enables planners to recommend COAs that achieve the commander's intent. Assured mobility emphasizes integrated proactive mobility, countermobility, and protection tasks to increase the probability of mission accomplishment.

3-69. While engineers are principal staff integrators for the assured mobility framework, all staff planners are essential to ensuring the effective application and integration of mobility, countermobility, and protection tasks. (See ATP 3-90.4 for more information on combined arms mobility.)

Mobility

3-70. *Mobility tasks* are those combined arms activities that mitigate the effects of obstacles to enable freedom of movement and maneuver (ATP 3-90.4). Mobility has six primary tasks:

- Conduct breaching.
- Conduct clearing (areas and routes).

Chapter 3

- Conduct gap crossing.
- Construct and maintain combat roads and trails.
- Construct and maintain forward airfields and landing zones.
- Conduct traffic management and enforcement.

3-71. Movement and maneuver along multiple axes requires significant coordinated planning and synchronization. Mobility is necessary for the execution of the offense. It mainly focuses on enabling friendly forces to move and maneuver freely. Commanders seek the capability to move, exploit, and pursue enemy forces decisively across a wide front. When attacking, commanders concentrate the effects of combat power at selected locations. This may require a unit to improve or construct combat trails through areas where routes do not exist. The surprise achieved by attacking through an area believed to be impassable may justify the effort expended in constructing these trails. Bypassing obstacles is the preferred method of overcoming obstacles.

3-72. Maintaining the offensive momentum of both armored and Stryker BCTs requires the careful planning and allocation of limited organic mobility capabilities. Maintaining the momentum of the offense requires an attacking force to bypass or breach obstacles as it encounters them. The preferred method of defeating a defended obstacle is by employing a hasty (in-stride) breach because it avoids the loss of time and momentum associated with planning, resourcing, and conducting a deliberate breach. An attacking unit makes a deliberate effort to capture bridges, beach and port exits, and other obstacles intact in order to control their use or destruction.

3-73. Wet (such as a river) and dry (such as an anti-vehicular ditch) gaps remain major obstacles during military operations. Wet gap crossings are among the most complex and risky combined arms operations that friendly maneuver forces encounter. Maneuver units conduct hasty crossings as a continuation of the attack whenever possible because the time needed to prepare for a gap crossing allows enemy forces more time to strengthen their defense. The size of a gap, as well as the enemy and friendly situations, dictates the specific TTP used in conducting a crossing.

3-74. Clearing operations are operations designed to clear or neutralize all mines and obstacles from a route or area. Clearing requires a combined arms force primarily built around engineer and explosive ordnance disposal capabilities. This combined arms team conducts clearing as single missions to open or reopen a route or area. Clearing may also be conducted on a recurring basis to support efforts to defeat recurring obstacles employed along routes and in areas. (See ATP 3-90.4 for additional information on mobility operations.)

Countermobility

3-75. *Countermobility operations* are those combined arms activities that use or enhance the effects of natural and man-made obstacles to deny enemy freedom of movement and maneuver (ATP 3-90.8). The primary purposes of countermobility are to shape enemy movement and maneuver and to prevent enemy forces from gaining a position of advantage. Countermobility supports the conduct of the offense, defense, and stability or defense support of civil authorities across the range of military operations.

3-76. Commanders perform countermobility tasks to isolate objectives and prevent enemy forces from repositioning, reinforcing, and counterattacking to support the offense. These tasks are also performed to provide flank protection and to deny or delay an enemy force's counterattack as the maneuver force progresses into the depth of the enemy force's defense. Commanders exploit terrain that offers natural flank protection to an attacking force, such as rivers or ridgelines. Swamps, canals, lakes, forests, and escarpments are natural terrain features that are easy to reinforce for flank security. Units can protect their flanks by denying enemy mobility corridors by building man-made obstacles, such as tank ditches, abatis, or road craters.

3-77. Countermobility during the offense requires rapid emplacement and flexibility. Obstacles deployed in the offense, to include scatterable mines, are normally emplaced by engineers, rotary-winged aircraft, or artillery. Engineers emplacing obstacles must keep pace with advancing maneuver forces and be prepared to emplace obstacles. Commanders consider likely enemy reactions to friendly actions and then plan how to block enemy avenues of approach or withdrawal. They also plan the use of obstacles to contain bypassed enemy elements, prevent enemy forces from withdrawing, and hinder enemy counterattacks.

3-78. Commanders integrate and synchronize countermobility considerations as part of their concepts of operations because obstacles can hinder both friendly and enemy maneuver. The control and accurate reporting of minefields and other tactical obstacles are vital. Control of obstacle initiation is necessary to prevent the premature activation of minefields and emplacement of obstacles. (See ATP 3-90.8 for information on obstacle integration and JP 3-15 for information on mine warfare.)

3-79. While conducting offensive operations, commanders place special emphasis on protection tasks related to survivability and detention operations. All units are responsible for improving their positions, regardless of role or location. *Survivability* is a quality or capability of military forces which permits them to avoid or withstand hostile actions or environmental conditions while retaining the ability to fulfill their primary mission (ATP 3-37.34). Survivability operations consist of four tasks which enhance the ability to avoid or withstand hostile actions by altering the physical environment: constructing fighting positions, constructing protective positions, hardening facilities, and employing camouflage and concealment. (See ATP 3-37.34 for additional information on survivability.)

Limited Visibility and Obscuration

3-80. The ability to fight at night, under limited-visibility conditions, or while employing obscuration is an important aspect of conducting maneuver. The performance of tasks and the conduct of operations under these conditions reduce risk of detection and enemy targeting. Commanders train their units under these conditions. Conducting offensive operations in these conditions can achieve surprise and make enemy visual target acquisition more difficult. They also take advantage of a friendly force's abilities to maneuver and employ fires under limited-visibility conditions.

3-81. Tasks performed or operations conducted in these three conditions require more planning and preparation time than similar tasks conducted during daylight. They require additional control measures. Leaders ensure that the night-vision and navigation systems required to maneuver under these conditions are available and functional. Leaders rehearse these operations before execution to ensure complete integration and synchronization of their plan.

3-82. An *obscurant* is material that decreases the level of energy available for the functions of seekers, trackers, and vision enhancement devices (ATP 3-11.50). Commanders employ obscuration in the offense to—
- Shape and control the operational environment.
- Protect friendly forces.
- Attack enemy forces.
- Deceive enemy commanders.

INTELLIGENCE

3-83. Conducting military operations requires intelligence products regarding threats and relevant aspects of an operational environment. These intelligence products enable commanders to—
- Understand enemy capabilities and intent.
- Visualize an operational environment.
- Plan operations.
- Identify and assess potential COAs.
- Properly direct forces.
- Employ effective tactics and techniques.
- Protect friendly forces.

3-84. Generating intelligence is a continuous task, driven by unit commanders. It begins before mission receipt and provides the knowledge required for the conduct of operations. Information is obtained through intelligence reach, data mining, academic studies, open-source intelligence, and other information sources. The information and intelligence obtained are refined for use in assessments, the intelligence preparation of the battlefield (IPB) process, and mission analysis.

3-85. Commanders and staffs use the IPB process to identify aspects of the AO or area of interest across relevant domains that affect enemy and friendly operations. The IPB process is collaborative and requires information from staff elements and subordinate units. All staff and subordinate elements use the results and products of the IPB process for planning. (See ADP 2-0 and ATP 2-01.3 for discussions of the IPB process.)

3-86. The intelligence process contributes to all warfighting functions. It helps commanders protect subordinate forces and identify key terrain, obstacles, and trafficability. IPB provides the basis for line of sight overlays and situation templates. Line of sight overlays help protect the force. If an enemy force cannot observe a friendly force, that enemy force cannot engage the friendly force with direct fire weapons. Situation templates also help protect the force. If they know how fast enemy forces can respond, commanders can sequence their operations, so they occur at times and places where enemy forces cannot respond effectively. Situation templates address terrain, mobility corridors, artillery range fans, movement times between enemy reserve assembly area locations and advancing friendly forces, and other related intelligence variables.

FIRES

3-87. The targeting process ensures the collective and coordinated use of Army indirect fires, air and missile defense, and joint fires to gain and maintain fire superiority. Commanders use a variety of methods and assets to achieve lethal and nonlethal effects on enemy forces to enable friendly maneuver.

Army Indirect Fires and Joint Fires in the Offense

3-88. The use of preparation fires, counterfires, suppression and destruction fires, information operations, cyberspace operations, and electronic warfare all contribute to gaining and maintaining fire superiority. Commanders use long-range artillery systems (cannon, rocket, and missile) and joint fires (such as naval surface fire support, air support, information operations, offensive cyberspace operations, and electronic attack) to engage enemy forces throughout the depth of their defensive positions.

3-89. Fire support planning is the continuing process of analyzing, allocating, and scheduling fires. It determines how commanders employ available fires, what types of targets to attack, what collection assets units use to acquire and track those targets, what assets it uses to attack those targets, and what assets verify effects on targets. This planning does not stop at the objective or LOA. Coordination among fire cells and the proper use of FSCMs at each echelon are critical in preventing fratricide while enabling the simultaneity of fires delivery with forces operating on the ground and in the air.

3-90. The fire support coordinator or chief of fires (depending on the echelon) integrates fires into a unit's scheme of maneuver for its commander. The fire support coordinator or chief of fires supports the unit's maneuver by planning preparation fires, harassing fires, interdiction fires, suppressive and destruction fires, and fires to support military deception activities. These fires can be time or event driven. The fire support coordinator or chief of fires plans fires on known and likely enemy positions. Successful massing of indirect fires, cyberspace effects, and joint fixed-wing attacks requires a fires cell that is proficient in tracking friendly indirect fire asset positions and knows weapons employment requirements. It also requires a tactical air control party proficient in the timely execution of close air support. Fire planning reconciles top-down planning and bottom-up refinement.

3-91. As an attacking force moves forward, preparation fires neutralize, suppress, or destroy enemy positions. Commanders assess the probable effects of preparation fires against losing a degree of surprise or increasing their vulnerability to counterfires when determining whether to fire an artillery preparation. Commanders may also decide to employ precision munitions against selected high-payoff targets to negate the requirement for long duration preparation fires using standard munitions.

3-92. A defending enemy force possessing artillery, rocket, cyberspace, and electronic warfare capabilities seeks to use any advantage to disrupt friendly command or control, fire support, information collection, and sustainment activities. Methods that an attacking force could employ when faced with a defending enemy force enjoying superior fire support capabilities include—
- Target selected enemy forces to enable the forward displacement of friendly fire support systems.
- Disperse attacking troops, systems, and supplies as much as is possible.

- Protect attacking troops, systems, and supplies by only moving them into attack positions at the last possible moment.
- Counter enemy target acquisition efforts by effectively using counter-reconnaissance and security operations, military deception, cover, and concealment.
- Target enemy command and control nodes to disrupt them.
- Exploit initial penetrations of enemy defensive positions to the maximum extent possible. (Overrunning enemy artillery systems, command and control nodes, and sustainment assets will seriously degrade a defending enemy force's combat power.)

The method or methods attacking commanders employ depend on the applicable mission variables.

3-93. Preparation fires are normally high-volume fires delivered over a short period to maximize surprise and shock effects. These preparation fires also include the conduct of electronic warfare and offensive cyberspace operations. They can continue while ground maneuver elements are moving or maneuvering during the conduct of the offense.

3-94. Artillery and mortars occupy positions that are well forward and within supporting range of the flanks of attacking maneuver forces to provide responsive indirect fires. Commanders consider the effect that movement has on the available amount of fire support. When facing an enemy with a highly sophisticated integrated fires complex, disaggregation of friendly artillery to the section level may be required for survivability. Commanders support their decisive operations by designating priority of fires. Their main efforts before their initiation of their decisive operation generally have priority of fires. They place coordinated fire lines as close to their units as possible without interfering with the maneuver of their forces. They plan on-order coordinated fire lines that shift as their forces move and maneuver. This allows the rapid engagement of targets beyond these coordinated fire lines by the maximum number of available systems.

3-95. The effective assignment of Army forward observers, joint fires observers, and target acquisition assets to quick fire networks facilitates responsive fires. Quick fire networks allow the lead observers to communicate directly with specific field artillery or mortar firing units. These communication arrangements enhance responsiveness through streamlined networks and focused priorities. Communications planning also includes the need for communications networks for the rapid clearing of targets for rotary- and fixed-wing attacks.

3-96. Commanders conduct information operations to support the offense with both lethal and nonlethal effects. Through their scheme of information operations, commanders establish objectives in the information environment and synchronize information-related capabilities to achieve these objectives through the creation of specific effects. Electronic warfare jamming resources and available supporting cyberspace assets concentrate on neutralizing enemy fire control, target acquisition, and information collection assets as a friendly force moves through an enemy's disruption zone and closes into an enemy's main defensive positions in the battle zone. Commanders use military deception to prevent an enemy force from determining the location and objective of a friendly decisive operation. In addition, intelligence sensors provide guidance to both friendly jammers and lethal indirect fire weapon systems, so attacking units can destroy enemy command and control nodes, reconnaissance and surveillance assets, artillery, and other high-payoff targets.

Air and Missile Defense

3-97. Commanders should never assume friendly air superiority. A ground force's primary air defense systems are joint fighter aircraft conducting offensive counterair operations. These systems are operated by the joint force air component commander. Air and missile defense systems include organic or attached mounted or dismounted maneuver short-range air defense systems. During mission analysis, commanders, informed by the air defense coordinator, determine the air threat and its effect on the operation. During offensive operations, commanders direct the positioning of available organic or supporting radars and short-range air defense systems to locations where they can best support the unit's attack in accordance with the critical and defended asset lists. The air defense and airspace management element in a unit staff ensures that it has communications with the appropriate air and missile defense organization's command post.

3-98. The supporting air and missile defense command post provides additional information to supported units, clarifying the air defense situation. This includes information on the engagement of air threats by the joint force air component commander and Army air defense systems. Attacking units concentrate on conducting passive air defense measures during offensive operations and supplement maneuver short-range air defense systems coverage with combined arms for air defense measures using organic direct fire systems against threat air systems. Passive air defense measures are an essential part of air and missile defense planning at all levels and reduce the effectiveness of the enemy air threat. Effective commanders include passive air defense measures in planning at all levels.

3-99. Commanders establish air defense priorities based on the concept of operations, scheme of maneuver, air situation, critical and defended asset lists, and the air defense priorities established by higher echelon headquarters. If commanders have Army air defense systems in direct support of their attack, their coverage is generally weighted toward their unit's decisive operation and establishing a protective corridor over the terrain traversed by units conducting that decisive operation. Targets selected to support tactical air defense efforts include—

- Enemy unmanned aircraft systems.
- Enemy rotary- and fixed-wing aircraft.
- Enemy facilities supporting enemy air operations, such as airfields, launch sites, logistic support facilities, forward arming and refueling points, and aerial command and control sites.

Enemy ground facilities are normally engaged by maneuver and fire support units and not air defense artillery units. (See FM 3-01 for additional information on air defense measures.)

SUSTAINMENT

3-100. Sustainment enables tactical momentum in the offense, and it requires detailed planning. Commanders attempt to take advantage of windows of opportunity and execute the offense with minimum advance warning time. Therefore, sustainment—logistics, personnel services, and health service support—planners and operators anticipate these events and maintain the flexibility to support an offensive plan accordingly. Sustainment commanders must act, rather than react, to support requirements. The existence of habitual support relationships facilitates the ability to anticipate.

Logistics

3-101. Logistics maintains the momentum of an attack by delivering supplies as far forward as possible. Commanders can use throughput distribution and preconfigured packages of essential items to help maintain offensive momentum and tempo. Commanders examine their unit's basic load to determine its adequacy to support an operation. The *basic load* is the quantity of supplies required to be on hand within, and moved by a unit or formation, expressed according to the wartime organization of the unit or formation and maintained at the prescribed levels (JP 4-09). Commanders determine the combat load—the supplies carried by individual Soldiers and combat vehicles. A unit's sustainment load consists of what remains of that unit's basic load once the combat load is subtracted. Unit tactical vehicles carry the sustainment load. Commanders also determine the supplies required for likely contingencies, such as enemy use of CBRN agents.

3-102. Logistic units and materiel remain close to a maneuver force to ensure short turnaround time for supplies and services. This includes uploading as much critical materiel—such as petroleum, oils, and lubricants (known as POL), water, and ammunition—as possible. Commanders conceal logistic preparations for an attack to deny enemy forces indications of their unit's tactical plans.

3-103. The availability of adequate supplies and transportation to sustain an operation becomes more critical as the operation progresses. Supply lines of communications (LOCs) lengthen, and the requirements for repair and replacement of weapon systems increase. Sustainment units in direct support of maneuver units must be as mobile as the forces they support. A way to provide continuous support is to task-organize elements of sustainment units or complete sustainment units with their supported maneuver formations as required by the mission variables.

3-104. A flexible and tailorable transportation system is necessary for widely dispersed forces and lengthening LOCs. Required capabilities include movement control, in-transit visibility of carried supplies, terminal operations, and transportation modes. Securing these LOCs and the units and convoys moving along them is critical.

3-105. Field maintenance assets move as far forward as the tactical situation allows to repair inoperable and damaged equipment as quickly as possible. Crews perform preventive checks and services as modified for the climate and terrain. Rapid battle damage assessment and repair is critical to sustaining an attack.

3-106. Establishing aerial resupply and forward logistic bases may be necessary to sustain maneuver operations conducted at great distance from a unit's sustaining base. This often occurs during an exploitation and pursuit.

3-107. Raids conducted by ground maneuver forces within the enemy force's support areas tend to be audacious, rapidly executed, and of short duration. Logistic support is normally minimal when units conduct raids. Units conducting raids should carry as much petroleum, oils, and lubricants and ammunition as possible and take advantage of any captured enemy supplies. Once a raiding force crosses its LD, only limited, emergency aerial resupply of critical supplies and aeromedical evacuation are feasible because of the absence of a secure ground LOC. Commanders must thoroughly plan for aerial resupply of a raiding force, since it entails greater risk than normal operations. Under these conditions, units typically destroy damaged equipment that is unable to maintain the pace of the operation.

Health Service Support

3-108. The burden on medical resources increases due to the intensity of offensive operations and the increased distances over which support is required as a force advances. Medical units must correspondingly anticipate large numbers of casualties over a large geographic area. The employment of weapons of mass destruction will greatly increase casualties. Mass casualty situations can exceed the capabilities of organic and direct support medical assets. To prevent this from occurring, planners should anticipate this possibility and coordinate with area support medical units for additional support. Additionally, units should plan and rehearse nonstandard casualty evacuation procedures. Effective management of mass casualty situations depends on established and rehearsed mass casualty plans and detailed medical planning. There are a number of other variables which can ensure the success of a unit's mass casualty response plan. These include—

- Coordination and synchronization of additional medical support and augmentation.
- Prior identification and designation of the projected casualty collection points.
- Quick location and clearance of the injured.
- Effective emergency medical treatment.
- Accurate triage and rapid medical evacuation of the injured to medical treatment facilities at the next higher role of care.

PROTECTION

3-109. Protection preserves combat power. Commanders address the twelve protection tasks during their planning, preparation, execution, and assessment of offensive operations. They protect their forces and critical assets by synchronizing, integrating, and organizing protection capabilities and resources. The synchronization and integration of area and local security tasks, operations security, air and missile defense, and cyberspace and electronic warfare operations is essential to protecting the force.

3-110. Various military organizations provide complementary and reinforcing protection capabilities in an economy-of-force role to protect LOCs, convoys, or critical fixed sites and radars. Bases and base clusters employ local security measures, but they may remain vulnerable to bypassed enemy forces. These forces may require commanders to employ tactical combat forces when their threat requires a friendly response beyond the capabilities of base and base cluster defense forces.

3-111. During the conduct offensive operations, commanders place special emphasis on protection tasks related to survivability and detention operations. All units are responsible for improving their positions, regardless of role or location.

3-112. Commanders ensure that their units can perform assigned tasks in CBRN environments. They establish, train, rehearse, and exercise their units under CBRN conditions before deploying into a theater of operations and during temporary lulls to build Soldier confidence and competence in these environments. Leaders and Soldiers know the challenges associated with wearing protective gear. Commanders integrate CBRN reconnaissance and surveillance into their overall information collection plans.

3-113. Army forces execute combined arms operations for countering weapons of mass destruction (known as CWMD) in an opportunistic manner during offensive operations when enemy forces present targets of opportunity. Integrated teams made up of maneuver forces and enablers conduct combined arms countering weapons of mass destruction at the tactical level. These teams provide integral, required capabilities to perform countering weapons of mass destruction tasks to curtail the research, development, possession, proliferation, use, and effects of weapons of mass destruction, related expertise, materials, technologies, and means of delivery. (See ATP 3-90.40 for more information on combined arms countering weapons of mass destruction.)

3-114. Units can expect to accumulate sizeable numbers of detainees during the conduct offensive operations. To facilitate collecting enemy tactical information, military intelligence personnel co-locate interrogation teams at detention facilities. (See FM 3-63 for additional information on detainee operations.)

TRANSITION

3-115. A transition occurs when a commander makes the assessment that units must change their focus from one element of decisive action to another. A commander halts offensive operations only when attacking units reach the echelon's LOA, achieve victory and the end of hostilities, reach a culminating point, or receive a change in mission from a higher echelon commander.

3-116. All types of offensive operations that do not achieve complete victory reach a culminating point when the balance of combat power shifts from the attacking force to the defending force. Units conducting offensive operations lose momentum and may culminate when—
- They suffer heavy losses of personnel and equipment.
- They encounter heavily defended areas they cannot bypass.
- The resupply of fuel, ammunition, and other supplies fails to keep up with expenditures.
- Soldiers become physically exhausted.
- Equipment repairs and personnel replacements do not keep pace with losses.
- The commander determines that advancing further is detrimental to the force. (Examples of this include moving out of mutual supporting distance with adjacent units or determining that the force lacks the enablers necessary to continue the advance.)

Attacking units may also slow or stop when reserves are not available to continue an advance, the defender receives reinforcements, or the defender counterattacks. Several of these causes may combine to halt an offense. When this occurs, the attacking unit can regain its momentum, but normally this only happens after difficult fighting, the commitment of additional forces, or an operational pause.

3-117. If commanders cannot achieve their objectives before subordinate forces reach their culminating points, they plan an operational pause to adjust the operation accordingly. Simultaneously, commanders attempt to prevent an enemy force from knowing when friendly forces become overextended.

TRANSITION TO DEFENSIVE OPERATIONS

3-118. Commanders retain greater flexibility for defensive operations if they begin preparations before the force culminates. This may allow commanders to dictate where they conduct defensive operations. Commanders can plan future activities to aid defensive operations, minimize vulnerability to attack, and facilitate renewal of offensive operations as a force transitions to branches or sequels of an ongoing operation. For example, some of a commander's subordinate units may move into battle positions before the entire unit terminates the offense. Commanders can echelon sustainment assets forward to establish a new echelon support area.

3-119. Commanders who anticipate a transition from offensive operations to defensive operations prepare orders to address when it occurs, what subordinate units will do, and which necessary control measures to implement. As a unit transitions from an offensive focus to a defensive focus, its commander—
- Maintains contact and surveillance of enemy forces, using a combination of reconnaissance units and surveillance assets to develop the information required to plan future actions.
- Establishes a security area, security force, and local security measures.

- Redeploys artillery assets to ensure the support of security forces.
- Redeploys forces for probable future employment.
- Maintains or regains contact with adjacent units in a contiguous AO and ensures that units remain capable of mutual support when operating in noncontiguous AOs.
- Shifts the engineer emphasis from mobility to countermobility and survivability.
- Consolidates and reorganizes.
- Explains the rationale for transitioning from the offense to the unit's leaders and Soldiers.

3-120. Commanders conduct reorganization and resupply concurrently with other transition activities. This requires a change in the sustainment effort. It shifts emphasis from ensuring a force's ability to move forward (including resupply of petroleum, oils, and lubricants, forward repair and maintenance, and replacing combat losses) to ensuring the force's ability to defend at a chosen location. A transition is often a time when units can perform equipment maintenance. Additional assets may also be available for casualty evacuation and medical treatment because of a reduction in tempo.

3-121. It is difficult to transition to the defense without prior planning. Defensive preparations which are not deliberately prepared are hasty and almost always initially characterized by severe time and resource constraints. Forces establishing a hasty defense may be dispersed and lacking combat power due to losses. Moreover, the shift to the defense requires a psychological adjustment. Soldiers who have become accustomed to advancing must now halt and fight defensively on often unfavorable terms.

3-122. If a commander determines that it is necessary to stop an offensive operation and conduct a retrograde, subordinate units may conduct an area defense from their current locations until their activities can be synchronized to conduct the retrograde operation. The amount of effort expended in establishing an area defense depends on the prevailing mission variables.

TRANSITION TO STABILITY OPERATIONS

3-123. At some point during an operation, units transition from one phase of the major operation or campaign plan to another and begin executing a sequel to their previous order the successful conduct of stability may be the decisive operation to a major operation or campaign. The transition to a focus on the conduct of stability from the conduct of the offense cannot be an afterthought. To assist in this transition to a stability focus, units continuously consolidate gains. Commanders actively consider activities necessary to consolidate gains while seeking to achieve their end state. It is the final exploitation of tactical success.

3-124. If a force achieves its objectives, and the situation makes focusing on defensive operations inappropriate, then commanders transition to a security and stability focus. The commander's intent and concept of operations drives the design and planning for security and stability. Generally, commanders focus on meeting the minimum-essential stability tasks by providing security and ensuring the provision of essential food, water, shelter, and medical treatment services to the civilian inhabitants in their AO. This occurs in coordination with any existing civil institutions and nongovernmental organizations before addressing the other stability concerns.

3-125. During this period of transition, there is a significant risk to the legitimacy of the mission. There exists a vacuum in the lull between fighting and establishing a secure environment. This is generally a result of reconfiguring a force from an operational force to an occupation force. Each context has its own specific governing laws and rules of engagement. As the force transitions, threats seek to establish systems and networks that circumvent the nascent security environment. Threats can take advantage by prolonging the transition. Denying threats safe havens and accounting for all the former enemies' combat resources enable friendly forces to limit the duration of this transitory period.

This page intentionally left blank.

Chapter 4
The Defense

This chapter discusses the basics of defensive operations. These basics include the purposes of the defense, characteristics of the defense, the three types of defensive operations, common defensive control measures, common defensive planning considerations, and transitions.

PURPOSES OF THE DEFENSE

4-1. While the offense is more decisive, the defense is usually stronger. However, the conduct of the defense alone normally cannot determine the outcome of battles. Army forces generally conduct the defense to create conditions favorable for the offense.

4-2. The purpose of the defense is to create conditions for the offense that allows Army forces to regain the initiative. Other reasons for conducting the defense include—
- Retaining decisive terrain or denying a vital area to an enemy.
- Attriting or fixing an enemy as a prelude to the offense.
- Countering enemy action.
- Increasing an enemy's vulnerability by forcing an enemy commander to concentrate subordinate forces.

4-3. A *defensive operation* is an operation to defeat an enemy attack, gain time, economize forces, and develop conditions favorable for offensive or stability operations (ADP 3-0). The inherent strengths of the defense are the defender's ability to occupy positions before an attack and use the available time to improve those defenses. A defending force stops improving its defensive preparations only when it retrogrades or begins to engage enemy forces. Even during combat, a defending force takes the opportunities afforded by lulls in action to improve its positions and repair combat damage.

4-4. A defending force does not wait passively to be attacked. A defending force aggressively seeks ways of attriting and weakening enemy forces before close combat begins. A defending force maneuvers to place enemy forces in a position of disadvantage and attacks those enemy forces at every opportunity. The static and mobile elements of a defense combine to deprive enemy forces of the initiative. A defending force contains enemy forces while seeking every opportunity to transition to the offense.

CHARACTERISTICS OF THE DEFENSE

4-5. Defending commanders strive to regain the initiative from attacking enemy forces. This is a primary feature of the defense. Disruption, flexibility, maneuver, mass and concentration, operations in depth, preparation, and security are all defensive characteristics used by commanders to regain the initiative. Their ability to synchronize their decisive, shaping, and sustaining operations greatly improves the probability of a successful defense.

DISRUPTION

4-6. Defending forces seek to disrupt attacks by employing actions that desynchronize an enemy force's preparations. Disruption actions include deceiving or destroying enemy reconnaissance forces, breaking up combat formations, separating echelons, and impeding an enemy force's ability to synchronize its combined arms. Defending forces conduct spoiling attacks to deny an enemy force's ability to focus combat power. They counterattack to deny an enemy force the ability to exploit. Defending forces employ electronic warfare

Chapter 4

and cyberspace assets in addition to lethal systems to target enemy command and control systems and disrupt enemy forces in depth by isolating forward echelons from their higher echelon headquarters.

FLEXIBILITY

4-7. Defensive operations require flexible plans that anticipate enemy actions and allocates resources accordingly. Commanders shift the main effort as required. They plan battle positions in depth and the use of reserves in spoiling attacks and counterattacks.

MANEUVER

4-8. Maneuver allows a defending force to achieve and exploit a position of advantage over an enemy force. As described in paragraphs 1-23 through 1-32, even in the defense there are elements of the offense. The defending force seeks opportunities to maneuver against the attacking force.

MASS AND CONCENTRATION

4-9. Defending forces seek to mass and concentrate effects against enemy forces. This action produces overwhelming combat power at specific locations to support their decisive operations. Defending forces can surrender ground to gain time for maneuver that allows them to mass and concentrate effects.

4-10. Commanders accept certain risk to mass effects at decisive points or for their main efforts. Concentrating forces increases the risk of large-scale losses from enemy fires and weapons of mass destruction. They mitigate this risk by using military deception and concealment to avoid detection of friendly troop concentrations by enemy intelligence, surveillance, and reconnaissance assets.

4-11. Commanders designate, retain, and when necessary reconstitute a reserve. They employ their reserve to exploit counterattack opportunities, regain local superiority, preserve the integrity of their defense, and prevent friendly culmination. They reconstitute their reserve from other forces when their reserve is committed.

OPERATIONS IN DEPTH

4-12. ***Operations in depth* is the simultaneous application of combat power throughout an area of operations**. Commanders plan their operations in depth. They create conditions by disrupting enemy long-range fires, sustainment, and command and control. These disruptions weaken enemy forces and prevent any early enemy successes. Operations in depth prevent enemy forces from maintaining their tempo. In the defense, commanders establish a security area and the main battle area (MBA) with its associated FEBA. (See paragraphs 4-31 and 4-33 for more information about the FEBA and MBA respectively.)

PREPARATION

4-13. Defending units prepare their AOs before attacking enemy forces arrive, or they establish the defense behind a force performing a security operation. Commanders employ forward and flank security forces to protect their defending forces from surprise and reduce the unknowns in any situation. Defending forces study the terrain, study enemy forces, and prepare engagement areas. They combine natural and man-made obstacles to canalize attacking forces into those engagement areas. Defending forces place information collection assets throughout their AOs to provide intelligence and early warning of enemy actions. They position combat multipliers, such as fires and sustainment assets, to support their defensive plans. Defending forces improve the survivability of their units by constructing field fortifications, using camouflage, and dispersing. Defending forces continue rehearsals and preparations until close combat begins.

SECURITY

4-14. Commanders secure their forces through the performance of security, protection, information operations, and cyberspace and electronic warfare tasks. Security may include the provision of area security for civilians, infrastructure, and LOCs. Security operations prevent enemy intelligence, surveillance, and reconnaissance assets from determining friendly locations, strengths, and weaknesses. These operations also provide early warning and continuously disrupt enemy attacks. They employ protection efforts to preserve combat power. This includes protecting their forces from attrition by using available air and missile defense assets. They conduct information operations to prevent civilian interference with their operations. They perform military deception, cyberspace, and electronic warfare to inaccurately portray friendly forces' locations, capabilities, and intentions to mislead enemy commanders and to deny those same enemy commanders the ability to use cyberspace and the electromagnetic spectrum.

TYPES OF DEFENSIVE OPERATIONS

4-15. Friendly forces use three types of defensive operations to deny enemy forces advantages:
- Area defense focuses on terrain.
- Mobile defense focuses on the movement of enemy forces.
- Retrograde focuses on the movement of friendly forces.

AREA DEFENSE

4-16. **The *area defense* is a type of defensive operation that concentrates on denying enemy forces access to designated terrain for a specific time rather than destroying the enemy outright**. The focus of an area defense is on retaining terrain where the bulk of a defending force positions itself in mutually supporting, prepared positions. Units maintain their positions and control the terrain between the position of enemy forces and the terrain they desire. The decisive operation focuses fires into engagement areas, possibly supplemented by a counterattack. Commanders can use their reserve to reinforce fires, add depth, block, or restore a position by counterattack; to seize the initiative; and to destroy enemy forces. Units at all echelons can conduct an area defense. The Battle of Kursk in July 1943 is a historical example of an area defense by the Soviets. (See FM 3-90-1 for a discussion of the advantages and disadvantages of the use of a defense in depth and a forward defense during the conduct of an area defense.)

MOBILE DEFENSE

4-17. **The *mobile defense* is a type of defensive operation that concentrates on the destruction or defeat of the enemy through a decisive attack by a striking force**. The mobile defense focuses on defeating or destroying enemy forces by allowing them to advance to a point where they are exposed to a decisive counterattack by a striking force. **The *striking force* is a dedicated counterattack force in a mobile defense constituted with the bulk of available combat power. A *fixing force* is a force designated to supplement the striking force by preventing the enemy from moving from a specific area for a specific time**. A fixing force supplements a striking force by holding attacking enemy forces in position, by canalizing attacking enemy forces into ambush areas, and by retaining areas from which to launch the striking force. German General Manstein's Donbas Operation in the Ukraine in February 1943 was a mobile defense.

4-18. A mobile defense requires an AO with considerable depth. Commanders shape their battlefields causing enemy forces to overextend their LOCs, expose their flanks, and dissipate their combat power. Commanders move friendly forces around and behind enemy forces to cut off and destroy them. Divisions and larger echelon formations normally execute mobile defenses. BCTs and maneuver battalions participate in a mobile defense as part of a fixing force or a striking force.

RETROGRADE

4-19. **The *retrograde* is a type of defensive operation that involves organized movement away from the enemy**. An enemy force may compel these operations, or a commander may perform them voluntarily. The higher echelon commander of a force executing a retrograde must approve the retrograde before its initiation. A retrograde is not conducted in isolation. It is always part of a larger scheme of maneuver designed to regain the initiative and defeat the enemy.

4-20. The three variations of the retrograde are delay, withdrawal, and retirement:

Chapter 4

- A *delay* **is when a force under pressure trades space for time by slowing down the enemy's momentum and inflicting maximum damage on enemy forces without becoming decisively engaged**. In delays, units yield ground to gain time while retaining flexibility and freedom of action to inflict the maximum damage on enemy forces.
- *Withdraw* **is to disengage from an enemy force and move in a direction away from the enemy**. Withdrawing units, whether all or part of a committed force, voluntarily disengage from an enemy force to preserve the withdrawing force or release it for a new mission.
- A *retirement* **is when a force out of contact moves away from the enemy**.

In each variation of a retrograde, a force not in contact with an enemy force moves to another location, normally by a tactical road march. In all variations of the retrograde, firm control of friendly maneuver elements is a prerequisite for success.

COMMON DEFENSIVE CONTROL MEASURES

4-21. Commanders control a defense by using control measures that provide the flexibility needed to allow defending commanders to concentrate combat power at the decisive point. They can use battle positions, direct fire control, and FSCMs in addition to other control measures to synchronize the employment of combat power. Commanders designate disengagement lines to trigger the displacement of subordinate forces.

BATTLE POSITIONS

4-22. **A *battle position* is a defensive location oriented on a likely enemy avenue of approach**. A battle position is not an AO. Battle positions symbols depict the locations and general orientations of defending ground maneuver forces. A commander's use of a battle position does not direct a subordinate to position that subordinate's entire force within its bounds. Units as large as battalion task forces and as small as squads or sections use battle positions. Commanders select positions based on terrain, enemy capabilities, and friendly capabilities. Commanders assign some or all subordinates battle positions. The unit occupying the battle position prepares fighting and survivability positions for its weapons systems, vehicles, Soldiers, and supplies to accomplish its mission.

4-23. Commanders assign subordinates to battle positions in situations when friendly forces need to retain a greater degree of control than that provided through only using an AO. This greater degree of control occurs because a commander controls maneuver outside the general location of the battle position. Multiple battle positions may be assigned to a single unit, which allows that unit to maneuver between battle positions. Commanders specify mission and engagement criteria to the unit assigned to a battle position. Security, supporting artillery, and sustainment forces typically operate outside a unit's battle position. Units occupying a battle position do not automatically have all the doctrinal responsibilities associated with being assigned an AO.

4-24. Units occupy or displace from battle positions as part of the overall plan. The commander assigning a unit to a battle position specifies when and under what conditions the unit displaces from the position. If a unit is ordered to defend a battle position, its commander has the option of moving off the battle position. If that unit is directed to retain a battle position, its commander needs to know the specific conditions that must exist before the unit can displace.

4-25. There are five kinds of battle positions:

- **The *primary position* is the position that covers the enemy's most likely avenue of approach into the area of operations**. It is the best position from which to accomplish the defensive mission, such as the overwatch of an engagement area to prevent enemy penetration.
- **An *alternate position* is a defensive position that the commander assigns to a unit or weapon system for occupation when the primary position becomes untenable or unsuitable for carrying out the assigned task**. The unit commander locates alternate positions so the occupants can continue to fulfill the original task, such as covering the same avenue of approach or engagement area as the primary position. These positions increase a defending force's survivability by allowing the defending force to engage the enemy force from multiple positions.

- **A *supplementary position* is a defensive position located within a unit's assigned area of operations that provides the best sectors of fire and defensive terrain along an avenue of approach that is not the primary avenue where the enemy is expected to attack.** An avenue of approach into a unit's AO from one of its flanks normally requires establishing supplementary positions to allow a unit or weapon system to engage enemy forces traveling along that avenue.
- **A *subsequent position* is a position that a unit expects to move to during the course of battle.** A defending unit may have a series of subsequent positions. Subsequent positions can also have primary, alternate, and supplementary positions associated with them.
- **A *strong point* is a heavily fortified battle position tied to a natural or reinforcing obstacle to create an anchor for the defense or to deny the enemy decisive or key terrain.** Commanders prepare a strong point for all-around defense. Commanders establish a strong point when anticipating enemy actions that will temporarily isolate a defending force retaining terrain critical to the overall defense.

4-26. When assigning battle positions, the commander always designates the primary battle position. Subordinate commanders designate and prepare alternate, supplementary, and subsequent positions as time and other resources permit, and if the terrain or situation requires them. Before assigning a strong point, commanders ensure that the strong point force has sufficient time and resources to construct the position. Constructing battle positions requires significant engineer support and Class I (primarily water for CBRN decontamination and consumption), Class IV (construction materials), and Class V (ammunition) supplies. A minimally effective strong point typically requires one day of effort from an engineer unit of the same size as the unit defending the strong point. Normally, companies and battalions occupy strong points, although brigades may construct them. Commanders do not normally establish strong points for units smaller than company size. This is because a platoon or squad cannot secure a perimeter large enough to contain all required assets and supplies.

DIRECT FIRE CONTROL MEASURES

4-27. Commanders engage an enemy force with all available fires when it enters a defending unit's engagement area. (See FM 3-90-1 for discussions on several direct fire control measures such as target reference points and trigger lines.)

DISENGAGEMENT LINE

4-28. **A *disengagement line* is a phase line located on identifiable terrain that, when crossed by the enemy, signals to defending elements that it is time to displace to their next position.** Commanders use disengagement lines in delays and defenses when they do not want a defending unit to become decisively engaged. Commanders establish criteria for a disengagement, such as number of enemy vehicles by type, friendly losses, or enemy movement to flanking locations. Commanders may designate multiple disengagement lines, one for type of each weapon system or subordinate unit.

ENGAGEMENT AREA

4-29. An *engagement area* is an area where the commander intends to contain and destroy an enemy force with the massed effects of all available weapons and supporting systems. In the defense commanders shape the enemy approach and steer enemy formations into engagement areas. They then concentrate overwhelming combat power in a focused area to defeat an enemy attack. The seven steps of engagement area development are identify all likely enemy avenues of approach, determine likely enemy schemes of maneuver, determine where to kill the enemy force, plan and integrate obstacles, emplace weapon systems, plan and integrate indirect fires, and rehearse.

FIRE SUPPORT COORDINATION MEASURES

4-30. Commanders try to engage an enemy force at extended ranges as the enemy's attack advances. To control indirect fires, commanders use permissive and restrictive FSCMs. Permissive FSCMs include the coordinated fire line, the FSCLs, and free-fire areas. Restrictive FSCMs include the airspace coordination area, no fire area, restrictive fire area, and restrictive fire lines. (See FM 3-90-1 and FM 3-09 for discussions

Chapter 4

on most of these FSCMs. See FM 3-52 for discussions on airspace coordination areas.) Commanders can also designate final protective fire (FPF). *Final protective fire* is an immediately available, prearranged barrier of fire designed to impede enemy movement across defensive lines or areas (JP 3-09.3).

FORWARD EDGE OF THE BATTLE AREA

4-31. The *forward edge of the battle area* is the foremost limits of a series of areas in which ground combat units are deployed to coordinate fire support, the positioning of forces, or the maneuver of units, excluding areas in which covering or screening forces are operating (JP 3-09.3). The Army uses a FEBA only during the defense. The FEBA is not a boundary, but it conveys the commander's intent. The FEBA shows the senior commander's planned limit for the effects of direct fires. It marks the foremost limits of the areas in which most ground combat units deploy, excluding the areas in which security forces are operating. MBA forces can temporarily move forward of the FEBA to expedite the retrograde operations of security forces. Commanders designate a FEBA to coordinate fire support and to help in the maneuver of subordinate forces. A phase line designating the forward most point of the MBA indicates the FEBA. Defending units must address this area in their scheme of maneuver and exchange information regarding tactical plans at contact points. (See figure 4-1.)

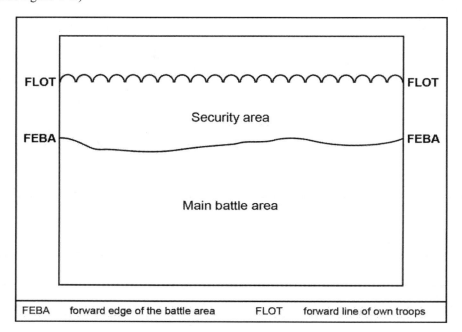

Figure 4-1. Defensive arrangement

FORWARD LINE OF OWN TROOPS

4-32. The *forward line of own troops* is a line that indicates the most forward positions of friendly forces in any kind of military operation at a specific time (JP 3-03). The FLOT normally identifies the forward location of covering or screening forces. In the defense, it may be beyond, at, or short of the FEBA. It does not apply to small, long-range reconnaissance assets and similar stay-behind forces. Friendly forces forward of the FLOT may have a restrictive FSCMs, such as a restrictive fire area, placed around them to prevent friendly fire incidents.

MAIN BATTLE AREA

4-33. **The *main battle area* is the area where the commander intends to deploy the bulk of the unit's combat power and conduct decisive operations to defeat an attacking enemy**. A defending commander's major advantage is the ability to select the ground on which the battle takes place. The natural defensive strength of a position determines the distribution of forces in relation to both frontage and depth. Defending units typically employ field fortifications and obstacles to reinforce the terrain's natural defensive aspects. The MBA includes the area where a defending force counterattacks that defeats or destroys enemy forces.

4-34. In contiguous operations, the MBA extends from the FEBA to the rear boundary of a specific echelon's subordinate units. Commanders locate subordinate unit boundaries along identifiable terrain features and extend them beyond the FLOT by establishing forward boundaries. Unit boundaries should not split avenues of approach or key terrain. Commanders select the MBA based on the products of the IPB process and their own analysis using the mission variables. The IPB anticipates how an enemy force will use the available avenues of approach.

SECURITY AREA

4-35. **A *security area* is that area occupied by a unit's security elements and includes the areas of influence of those security elements**. It may be located as necessary to the front, flanks, or rear of a protected unit, facility, or location. Forces in a security area furnish information on an enemy force; delay, deceive, and disrupt that enemy force; and conduct counterreconnaissance. All units perform security operations within their AOs, including the support area, to deny enemy reconnaissance and otherwise protect the force. Units implement security operations and other information protection measures to deny the enemy force information about friendly dispositions.

4-36. Commanders conduct security operations to provide their forces time and space to react to the approach of enemy forces by causing the enemy to deploy prematurely. This reveals the enemy forces' main effort and which of the available avenues of approach the enemy is using. Commanders conduct security operations to conceal the location of their main battle positions, prevent enemy observation of friendly preparations and positions, and prevent enemy forces from delivering observed fire on these positions. Commanders can offset an attacker's inherent advantage of initiative regarding the time, place, plan, direction, strength, and composition of the attack by forcing that enemy to attack into unexpected prepared defenses. They counter enemy ground and air reconnaissance activities through both active and passive measures. Commanders must not permit enemy reconnaissance and surveillance assets to determine the precise location and strength of defensive positions, obstacles, engagement areas, and reserves.

COMMON DEFENSIVE PLANNING CONSIDERATIONS

4-37. The defense is more effective when commanders and staffs have adequate time to thoroughly plan and prepare defensive positions. Lack of preparation time may cause a commander to maintain a larger-than-normal reserve or accept greater risk. All units must be capable of mounting a defense with minimal preparation. A defending commander can increase the effectiveness of the security area, establish additional alternate and supplementary positions, refine the defensive plan including branches and sequels, conduct defensive rehearsals, and maintain vehicles and personnel.

4-38. To gain time to organize a defense, commanders may order the security force to conduct a delay while the main body disengages and moves to more advantageous positions. The security force must know how long it needs to delay enemy forces for the main body to prepare its defense, and it must be task-organized to conduct a delay.

4-39. When an attack begins, a defending commander yields the initiative to enemy forces. Defending forces maintain security and disrupt enemy attacks at every opportunity. Defending commanders disrupt enemy attacks by using long-range fires to reduce the impact of the attacking enemy forces' initial blows and start wresting the initiative from enemy forces. Defending forces draw enemy forces into engagement areas where they can initiate combat on favorable terms. Commanders surprise enemy forces with concentrated and integrated fires against exposed enemy formations from concealed and protected positions. They then counterattack enemy forces, preferably when those enemy forces are most vulnerable to friendly capabilities. They exploit small tactical successes and opportunities to disrupt an attacker's momentum.

4-40. Defending forces do not have to kill every enemy soldier or destroy every combat system to accomplish their mission. They only have to eliminate the enemy force's ability to synchronize a combined arms team or break the enemy's capacity to fight. Those events signal a transition that affords defending commanders the opportunity to seize the initiative and transition to the offense.

Chapter 4

4-41. The common defensive planning considerations addressed in paragraphs 4-42 through 4-110 apply to all types of defensive operations. These considerations are in addition to those common offensive planning considerations introduced in chapter 3, when appropriately modified for the defense. Defensive synchronization is normally the result of detailed planning and preparation among the various units participating in defensive operations. While these activities may be separated in time and space, they are synchronized if enemy forces feel their combined consequences decisive times and places. The defense is a mix of static and dynamic actions. As an operation evolves, the defending commander prepares to shift main and supporting efforts and keep an enemy force off balance.

COMMAND AND CONTROL

4-42. The command and control considerations for the offense discussed in paragraphs 3-42 through 3-55 also apply to the defense. The commander's intent and mission determine the concept of operations, scheme of maneuver, and allocation of available resources and priorities.

4-43. Important command and control principles include mission orders, disciplined initiative, and commander's intent. Mission orders are the commander's directives that emphasize the results to be attained, not how they are to be achieved. Disciplined initiative is action in the absence of orders to react to the enemy's unforeseen actions, a new or more serious threat, or an opportunity that offers a greater chance of success than the original COA. Commanders rely on their subordinates to take their own initiative to adjust to the new situation and achieve their commander's intent. The commander's intent defines the limits within which subordinates may exercise their initiative. It gives subordinates the confidence to apply their judgment in ambiguous situations because they know the mission's purpose, key tasks, and desired end state.

4-44. A defensive mission generally imposes few restrictions on a defending commander. It allows freedom of maneuver within assigned boundaries, but it requires commanders to prevent enemy penetration of their rear boundary. Defending an AO is a typical mission for battalion and higher-echelon units. This mission allows commanders to distribute forces to advantageously use the terrain and plan engagement areas that integrate direct and indirect fires. Commanders ensure that subordinate unit defensive plans are compatible and that control measures, such as contact points and phase lines, are sufficient for flank and rear coordination when assigning AOs. The defensive plan addresses what happens when friendly forces succeed and gain an opportunity to transition from defensive operations to offensive operations.

4-45. Because an enemy force has the initiative, the defending commander frequently has to shift main and supporting efforts within the unit's shaping operations to contain the enemy's attack until the defending force can seize the initiative. This may require the commander to adjust subordinate unit AOs, repeatedly commit and reconstitute the reserve, and modify the original plan.

4-46. Commanders may change task organization to respond to an existing or a projected situation, such as forming a detachment left in contact before conducting a withdrawal. Commanders of recently reorganized units place special attention on ensuring that each element understands the unit's overall mission. This requires commanders to ensure that objectives are synchronized and subordinates understand their control measures, movement routes, defensive positions, fire support plans, and specifically assigned tasks. It also requires specifying the standard operating procedures that each element of a task-organized unit employs. Synchronizing and integrating task-organized elements results in more effective employment of available combat power.

4-47. An enemy force often attacks along the boundaries of defending units to break through the MBA. Therefore, it is extremely important for commanders at every echelon to ensure their defense is properly coordinated with flanking and supporting units. When possible, commanders coordinate through personal visits to subordinate commanders on the ground. Their staffs rapidly transmit coordination decisions to all concerned.

4-48. Since command posts and communications nodes tend to be relatively static in the defense, commanders place them in hardened areas or protective terrain to reduce their electronic and visual signatures. Command posts remain capable of rapidly relocating in response to battlefield developments.

4-49. As with the offense, commanders conduct information operations to support the defense. Through their scheme of information operations, commanders establish objectives in the information environment and synchronize information-related capabilities to achieve these objectives and create specific effects. Commonly synchronized information-related capabilities to support the defense include cyberspace operations, electronic warfare, military deception, military information support operations, and operations security.

MOVEMENT AND MANEUVER

4-50. Defending commanders seek to defeat the attacks of enemy forces by attriting those forces with repeated, unexpected engagements before they conduct their final assaults on friendly defensive positions. Enemy forces attempt to withdraw or transition to the defense in the face of friendly counterattacks once their attacks fail. If an enemy force succeeds in overrunning a key defensive position, that defending friendly unit counterattacks to restore defensive integrity before that enemy force can either organize that position for defense or exploit its success.

Exploit the Advantages of Terrain

4-51. Defending commanders exploit the advantages of occupying the terrain where an engagement will occur. A defending force engages an attacker from locations that give that defending force an advantage. Defensive positions in the MBA make use of existing and reinforcing obstacles. Commanders may shape the battlefield by defending in one area to deny terrain to an enemy force while delaying in another area. This is to deceive an enemy commander into believing that an attacking enemy force has achieved success.

4-52. Generally, defending forces have the advantage of preparing the terrain by reinforcing natural obstacles, fortifying positions, and rehearsing operations. (See ATP 3-90.8 for guidance on integrating obstacles into engagement areas and defensive positions.)

4-53. Terrain features that favor the defense include—
- A series of parallel ridges across the line of hostile advance.
- Unfordable streams, swamps, lakes, and other obstacles on the front and flanks.
- High ground with good observation and long-range fields of fire.
- Concealed movement routes immediately behind defensive positions.
- A limited road network in front of the line of contact to confine an enemy force to predictable avenues of approach.
- A good road network behind the line of contact that allows commanders to reposition forces as a battle progresses.

4-54. Depending on the mission variables, units can conduct survivability moves between their primary, alternate, and supplementary positions. **A *survivability move* is a move that involves rapidly displacing a unit, command post, or facility in response to direct and indirect fires, the approach of a threat or as a proactive measure based on intelligence, meteorological data, and risk assessment of enemy capabilities and intentions.** A survivability move includes those movements based on the impending employment of weapons of mass destruction.

Disrupt the Enemy Attack at Every Opportunity

4-55. The defending force conducts operations in multiple domains to disrupt an enemy commander's plan and destroy key units and assets. Particularly the defending force seeks to degrade enemy forces' command and control capabilities and integrated fires complex as well as to destroy their reserve. This compels early enemy culmination and allows the defending force to regain the initiative. The defending force conducts spoiling attacks to disrupt enemy troop concentrations and attack preparations. The defending force rapidly counterattacks an enemy success with its reserve, the forces at hand, or a striking force before the enemy force can exploit that success.

Mass the Effects of Combat Power

4-56. The decisive operation can be tied to a geographical location or against an enemy force. In an area defense, defending units use engagement areas to concentrate combat power from mutually supporting positions in selected engagement areas. In a mobile defense, commanders use a striking force to generate overwhelming combat power at the decisive point. Commanders can also mass effects by committing the reserve. Commanders use economy of force measures in areas that do not involve the decisive operation.

Armored and Stryker Forces

4-57. When most of a defending force consists of units equipped with armored combat vehicles, commanders can conduct a defense designed to take advantage of the tactical mobility and protection offered by those systems. Combat vehicles provide defending forces with the capability to maneuver to delay the advance of a strong enemy force and then immediately change from a dynamic to a static defense or counterattack. Defending forces equipped with armored combat vehicles are well suited for use as security and MBA forces. They are more suited for operations within a chemical, biological, radiological, and nuclear (CBRN) contaminated environment than dismounted infantry forces because of their built-in CBRN overpressure protection.

Dismounted Infantry Forces

4-58. Dismounted infantry forces facing an armored enemy force are primarily used in static roles within the MBA or in security roles within their echelon support and consolidation areas. When facing armored enemy forces, dismounted infantry forces are most effective when fighting from prepared defenses or in close terrain, such as swamps, woods, hilly and mountainous areas, and urban areas. From those positions they can take advantage of their foot mobility and short-range infantry and anti-armor weapons.

4-59. Commanders use airborne and air assault units in the same manner as they use other infantry forces once those units deploy into their landing zones. However, there may be challenges extracting them, particularly if those units come into direct contact with an enemy force. Because of its mobility and potential reaction speed, an airborne or air assault force is often well suited for a reserve role during the defense. Its tasks might include—

- Rapid reinforcement of a threatened position.
- Occupation of a blocking position, possibly in conjunction with existing defensive positions.
- Reinforcement of encircled friendly forces.
- Flank protection.

Aviation Forces

4-60. Aviation forces with their mix of manned and unmanned systems are particularly valuable in the defense because of their speed, mobility, and versatility. Their tasks can include—

- Conducting intelligence, surveillance, and reconnaissance, as part of information collection.
- Performing security operations.
- Conducting shaping operations or supporting efforts to establish the necessary conditions for decisive operations by other forces or the main effort through attriting, disrupting, and delaying the enemy.
- Conducting counterattacks and spoiling attacks.
- Controlling ground for limited periods where a commander does not wish to irrevocably commit ground forces; for example, forward of an executed obstacle.
- Countering enemy penetrations.
- Closing gaps in a defensive plan before the arrival of ground maneuver forces.
- Facilitating the disengagement of ground forces.
- Countering enemy activities in the echelon support areas, in particular enemy airborne or air assault forces.
- Resupplying a defending force or facilitating casualty evacuation.
- Assisting in the countermobility effort by employing minefields.

Ensure Mutual Support

4-61. Mutual support exists when positions and units support each other by direct and indirect fires, thus preventing an enemy force from attacking one position without being subjected to fire from one or more adjacent positions. Mutual support increases the strength of all defensive positions, prevents defeat in detail, and helps prevent enemy infiltration between positions. Battle positions achieve the maximum degree of mutual support when they are located to observe or monitor the ground between positions or when they conduct patrols to prevent any enemy infiltration. At night or during periods of limited visibility, commanders may position small units closer together to retain the advantages of mutual support. Unit leaders must coordinate the nature and extent of their mutual support.

Mobility

4-62. During a defense, mobility tasks include breaching obstacles, clearing routes, and constructing and maintaining combat roads and trails to support counterattacks. Mobility tasks are those combined arms activities that mitigate the effects of obstacles to enable freedom of movement and maneuver. Engineer units usually perform these tasks. Enemy fires and friendly use accelerate the normal wear on routes. Engineers maintain the trafficability of those routes. Enemy fires may necessitate deploying engineer equipment, such as assault bridging and bulldozers, forward. During a counterattack, engineer breaching systems open closed lanes or breach hasty minefields placed by a retrograding enemy force.

4-63. Commanders establish the priority of mobility support based on the mission variables. This support consists mainly of reducing obstacles and improving or constructing combat roads and trails to allow tactical support vehicles to accompany combat vehicles. Commanders coordinate carefully to ensure that units leave lanes or gaps in their obstacles that allow for the repositioning of main body units and the commitment of the counterattacking force. CBRN reconnaissance systems also contribute to a force's mobility in a contaminated environment by marking contaminated and clean routes as well as providing CBRN expertise while developing alternate COAs.

Countermobility

4-64. Commanders designate obstacle zones, belts, and groups depending on their authority. When planning obstacles, commanders and staffs also consider future operations. Commanders design obstacles for current operations so they do not hinder planned future operations. Any commander authorized to employ obstacles can designate certain obstacles to shape the battlefield. There are two categories of reinforcing obstacles: tactical and protective. Tactical obstacles shape enemy maneuver to maximize the effects of fires. Tactical obstacles deny the ability of a force to move, mass, and reinforce; therefore, they affect the tempo of operations. There are three types of tactical obstacles: directed, situational, and reserved. Commanders employ protective obstacles to protect people, equipment, supplies, and facilities against threats. Protective obstacles have two roles, defense or security.

4-65. Obstacles can provide additional protection from enemy attacks by forcing an enemy force to spend time and resources to breach or bypass them. Effective obstacles block, turn, fix, or disrupt, forcing an enemy to attempt to breach or bypass them. A commander integrates reinforcing obstacles with existing obstacles to halt or slow enemy movement, canalize enemy movement into engagement areas, and protect friendly positions and maneuver. The primary purpose for integrating obstacles with fires is to enhance the effectiveness of those fires. Obstacles that are not covered by fire generally disrupt only the leading elements of an attacking force for a short time. When possible, units conceal obstacles from hostile observation. They coordinate obstacle plans with adjacent units and conform to the obstacle zone or belts of higher echelons.

4-66. Commanders designate the unit responsible for creating and overwatching each obstacle. Commanders may retain execution authority for some obstacles—called reserved obstacles—or restrict the use of some types of obstacles to allow other battlefield activities to occur. All units must know which gaps or lanes—through obstacles and crossing sites—to keep open for movements, as well as the firing and self-destruct times of scatterable mines to prevent delays in movement. Commanders must be specific and clear in their orders for executing reserved obstacles and closing lanes. As each lane closes, the closing unit reports the lane's closure to prevent displacing units from moving into active obstacle areas.

4-67. Commanders at all echelons track defensive preparations, such as establishing Class IV and V supply points and start or completion times of obstacle belts and groups. Commanders plan how units will restore obstacles that an enemy force has breached. Commanders use artillery, air, or ground systems to reseed minefields. Given time and resources, a defending force constructs additional obstacles in depth, paying special attention to its assailable flanks and rear. (See ATP 3-90.8 for additional information about obstacles and obstacle integration.)

Enemy Airborne and Air Assault Attacks

4-68. Defeating an enemy airborne or air assault attack begins with a good IPB process to determine the enemy force's capabilities to conduct vertical envelopment and to identify enemy airfields, pickup zones, drop zones, and landing zones. Armed with an appreciation of an enemy force's capability to conduct vertical envelopment, commanders take steps to counterattack enemy forces before they launch, during their movement to the drop zone, or at the landing zone. Commanders may request joint offensive and defensive counterair support. After prioritizing the risk of each potential drop or landing zone to the operation, commanders establish surveillance of these areas to alert defending forces if an enemy insertion takes place. Units also sight their weapons to cover the most probable drop and landing zones. The fire support plan includes these zones in its target list for area fires munitions and scatterable munitions. Defending forces emplace obstacles in these locations and impede avenues of approach to critical friendly installations and activities as part of their countermobility and survivability efforts.

4-69. If enemy forces succeed in landing, a defending force contains and counterattacks them before they become organized and are reinforced. Friendly field artillery and attack helicopters must quickly engage enemy forces to take advantage of the concentration of targets in landing and drop zones. Joint fires can also be employed against such insertion areas. Available base and base cluster defense and response forces keep the enemy force under observation, designating targets for available fires. If more enemy troops land and consolidate, base cluster defense forces and the quick response force try to fix that enemy force to allow a tactical combat force to counterattack. Defending commanders may need to commit their reserve if an enemy force is too large for their tactical combat force to reduce.

Limited Visibility and Obscuration

4-70. An attacking enemy force can be expected to create or take advantage of limited visibility conditions. Normally, a defending commander can expect an attacker taking advantage of these conditions to—
- Conduct reconnaissance to locate a defender's weapons, obstacles, and positions.
- Breach or reduce defensive obstacles.
- Infiltrate through gaps in a defender's coverage caused by reduced target acquisition ranges.

4-71. Two limited visibility conditions exist: those which mechanical aids, such as thermal sights, can overcome or partially overcome and those which mechanical aids cannot overcome. The first category includes darkness. The second category includes dense battlefield dust, obscurants, heavy rain, snow, fog, or any other conditions which cannot be at least partially overcome by artificial illumination, image intensification, radar, or other sensors. In this case, defending units may need to move closer to the avenues of approach they are guarding. Sensors may still be of some value in these conditions.

4-72. Commanders use obscurants to disrupt an enemy force's assault or movement formations and to deny an enemy force's use of target acquisition optics, visual navigation aids, air avenues of approach, landing zones, and drop zones. Obscurants create gaps in enemy formations by separating or isolating attacking units and disrupting their planned movement. Obscurants affect both friendly and enemy forces.

INTELLIGENCE

4-73. Just as in the offense, intelligence collection is continuous. Intelligence officers, in coordination with the rest of the staff, develop a synchronized and integrated information collection plan that satisfies the unit commander's maneuver, targeting, and information requirements. These requirements in the defense are similar to those in the offense. Intelligence analysis helps commanders decide on the precise time and place to counterattack.

4-74. During planning, commanders use intelligence products to identify probable enemy objectives and approaches. From those probable objectives and approaches they develop named areas of interest and targeted areas of interest. In a defense, IPB should be able to determine an enemy force's strength, COAs, and the location of enemy follow-on forces. IPB products also identify cyberspace activities, cross-domain capabilities, patterns of enemy operations and the enemy force's vulnerabilities to counterattack, interdiction, electronic warfare, air attacks, and canalization by obstacles. Commanders study an enemy force's capability to conduct air attacks against friendly forces, insert forces behind friendly units, employ CBRN and explosive weapons or devices, and employ asymmetric or unconventional forces and tactics. The intelligence staff also evaluates how soon enemy follow-on forces can be committed. Defending commanders can then decide where to arrange their forces to defend and shape the battlefield.

4-75. Commanders designate targeted areas of interest and named areas of interest as necessary. Commanders determine the most advantageous area for an enemy force's main attack as well as other military aspects of terrain, including observation and fields of fire, avenues of approach, key terrain, obstacles, and cover and concealment. (See ATP 3-34.80 for a detailed discussion of observation and fields of fire, avenues of approach, key terrain, obstacles, and cover and concealment.) A defending unit continuously performs information collection tasks during a battle so that the defending commander can make the appropriate decisions and adjustments to the defense.

4-76. Some information collection assets are susceptible to loss. Defensive plans must also address the sustainment, replacement, and reconstitution of information collection assets throughout the execution of a defense.

FIRES

4-77. The targeting process ensures the collective and coordinated use of Army indirect and joint fires to gain and maintain fire superiority throughout defensive operations. In the defense, commanders use fires to neutralize, suppress, or destroy enemy forces. Commanders can also use fires to delay or disrupt an enemy force's ability to execute a given COA and to enhance the effects of massed direct fires or the employment of scatterable munitions.

Army Indirect Fires and Joint Fires in the Defense

4-78. A defending force is less effective when an attacking enemy force can deploy in combat formations within the MBA. A defending force is more effective if it can locate and attack enemy forces while enemy forces are stationary and concentrated in assembly areas or advancing along LOCs. To engage enemy forces in vulnerable locations, a defending force must effectively employ available indirect and joint fires throughout its AO. A defending force must be closely linked to target acquisition means, including information collection assets.

4-79. As defensive plans develop, commanders visualize how to synchronize, coordinate, and distribute the effects of indirect and direct fires at decisive times and places. All elements in the fire support chain—from joint fires observers and platoon forward observers in fire support teams to the echelon fires cell, including the supporting tactical air control party and the supporting fires units—must understand the commander's intent, the scheme of maneuver, and the obstacle plan. A defender's ability to mass fires quickly and then rapidly reposition forces is a major factor in disrupting the enemy. Commanders place permissive FSCMs as close as possible to friendly positions to enable the rapid engagement of attacking enemy forces by indirect and joint fires. Commanders coordinate the massing of fire effects on enemy targets concentrated at obstacles and other choke points before they can disperse. Proper distribution of fires prevents the massing of enemy combat power at these points and ensures that friendly forces destroy or neutralize high-payoff targets without wasting assets through repetitive engagements by multiple friendly systems.

4-80. Fire support assets continue to target enemy combat units to force them to deploy once an engagement moves into the MBA. At the same time, fire support assets inflict casualties, disrupt the cohesion of an enemy force's attack, and impede an enemy force's ability to mass combat power. Commanders take advantage of the range and flexibility of fire support weapons to mass fires at critical points, such as obstacles and engagement areas, to slow and canalize an enemy force to provide better targets for direct fire systems. Fire support systems cover barriers, gaps, and open areas within the MBA.

Chapter 4

4-81. Units conduct defensive operations and designate FPFs for each of their supporting artillery units and mortar platoons. Both direct and indirect-fire weapons can provide FPFs. A direct fire weapon system's final protective line is a form of FPFs. Commanders can only assign each weapon, firing battery, or platoon a single FPF. An FPF is a priority target for that weapon or unit, and those weapons or units are laid on that target when they are not engaged in other fire missions. When an enemy force initiates its final assault into a defensive position, a defending unit initiates its FPFs.

Air and Missile Defense

4-82. Army air defense artillery forces operate interdependently with other elements of a joint and multinational team by providing air and missile defense. They contribute to the deterrence or defeat of enemy aerial threats by protecting the force, protecting high-value assets, and enabling a force's freedom to operate. This mission is normally accomplished within a joint theater-wide structure and requires integration and close coordination between Army air defense artillery forces and other counterair forces.

4-83. Freedom of movement is essential to a successful defense. During large-scale combat operations, most friendly forces will not initially operate under the protection of air superiority. The joint force commander normally seeks to gain and maintain air superiority as quickly as possible to allow all friendly forces, not just ground forces, to operate without prohibitive interference from enemy air and missile threats. This counterair mission integrates both offensive operations and defensive operations by all joint force components. In an environment where air and missile threats exist, a defending ground force operates within a joint counterair operation designed to attain the degree of air superiority required by the joint force commander to accomplish the mission.

4-84. Ground commanders mitigate the risk of air and missile attack through various activities. These activities include camouflage, concealment, military deception, dispersion, redundancy, and protective construction. These activities improve unit survivability by reducing the likelihood of being detected and targeted from the air and by mitigating the potential effects of air surveillance and attack. Units improve survivability by detecting air and missile launches, predicting impact points, providing threat identification, and disseminating early warning.

SUSTAINMENT

4-85. Commanders address several unique sustainment considerations in the defensive plan. Priorities for replenishment normally include ammunition and materiel to construct obstacles and defensive positions. There is usually a reduced need for bulk fuel. Some situations may have an increased demand for decontaminants and CBRN collective and personal protective equipment. Commanders consider stockpiling or caching ammunition and limited amounts of petroleum products in centrally located positions within the MBA. Commanders plan to destroy those stocks if necessary as part of denial operations. The supply of obstacle materials in a defense can be a significant problem that requires detailed coordination and long lead times. Commanders consider the transportation and manpower required in obtaining, moving, and uncrating barrier material and obstacle creating munitions.

4-86. Sustainment unit commanders and sustainment staff officers understand their supported commander's intent. They establish support priorities in accordance with that intent and plan sustainment operations to ensure support for the overall operation. Commanders also address sustainment during branches and sequels to a defensive plan, such as a counterattack into the flank of an adjacent unit. This allows sustainment units to anticipate the needs of the maneuver units they support.

4-87. Maneuver units resupply regularly in case an enemy breakthrough disrupts sustainment. The sustainment enterprise may deliver combat-configured loads to its maneuver units. Combat-configured loads are typically packages of potable and non-potable water, CBRN defense supplies, barrier materials, ammunition, petroleum, oil, and lubricants (collectively known as POL), medical supplies, and repair parts tailored to a specific size unit. Sustainment organizations resupply their supported maneuver units until those maneuver forces request otherwise. Commanders use information systems to accurately tailor these combat-configured loads to the demands of supported maneuver units.

4-88. Commanders may need to infiltrate resupply vehicles to reduce detection chances when an enemy force possesses a significant air, satellite, or unmanned aircraft capability. Commanders may also use military deception, camouflage, concealment, and obscurants to help conceal logistic operations.

4-89. Terrain management is a critical consideration when establishing bases and base clusters in the support area. Commanders position each sustainment unit where it can best fulfill its support tasks while using minimal resources to maintain security in conjunction with other units located in an echelon support area. In contiguous operations, commanders position echelon sustainment facilities farther away from the FEBA in a defense than in the offense to avoid interfering with the movement of units between battle positions or the forward movement of counterattack forces. Commanders locate these assets far enough behind friendly lines that likely enemy advances will not compel the relocation of critical sustainment capabilities at inopportune times. However, those sustainment capabilities supporting a unit must be close enough to provide responsive support. In noncontiguous operations, commanders position sustainment assets in bases and base clusters within the perimeters of ground maneuver units to provide security and avoid interrupting their sustainment functions. Commanders distribute sustainment units with similar functions throughout the defensive area in both environments. This distribution allows commanders to designate one sustainment unit to pick up the workload of a displacing second sustainment unit until the second sustainment unit is once again operational. (See ATP 3-91 for a discussion of the use of bases and base clusters within the division support area.)

4-90. A defending commander provides maintenance support as far forward as possible at maintenance collection points to reduce the need to evacuate equipment. The goal of the maintenance effort is to fix as far forward as possible damaged systems that can be quickly returned to a unit in combat-ready condition. Commanders ensure that multifunctional forward logistic elements contain the maximum variety of maintenance personnel with appropriate equipment, such as repair sets, kits, and outfits, to rapidly repair weapon systems.

4-91. Medical support associated with the defense anticipates significant casualties, just as in the offense. Commanders plan to augment available ambulances for mass casualty situations. Units plan for mass casualties and have evacuation plans, including casualty collection points and ambulance exchange points, and account for the use of both standard and nonstandard air and ground evacuation platforms.

PROTECTION

4-92. In defensive operations, commanders protect forces and critical assets by synchronizing, integrating, and organizing protection capabilities and resources. Commanders incorporate available protection capabilities as they understand and visualize threats and hazards in an operational environment. Commanders then apply the elements of combat power to prevent or mitigate these threats or hazards from negatively impacting friendly operations. Commanders use decision support tools and analysis to assess a unit's critical assets and key vulnerabilities. (See ADP 3-37 for additional information on protection.)

4-93. In defensive operations, commanders protect forces and critical assets by performing security operations. Forces providing security in a defense can deter, detect, or defeat enemy reconnaissance efforts while creating standoff distances from enemy direct- and indirect-fire systems. Commanders secure the movement of combat trains and protect cached commodities.

4-94. Commanders clearly define responsibilities for the security of units within the support area. This requires assigning an individual responsibility for defensive planning and risk mitigation in that support area. That individual can designate the commanders of tenant units within support areas as base and base cluster commanders (except medical corps officers). Base and base cluster commanders are responsible for the local security of their respective bases and base clusters. A commander responsible for a support area can also designate protection standards and defensive readiness conditions for tenant units and units transiting the area. Higher protection standards may impact the ability of those supporting sustainment units to accomplish their primary missions to support the operations of maneuver and other forces. The support area commander coordinates to mitigate the effects of performing security operations on the primary functions of units located within an echelon support area. (There are two approaches for arraying base camps: dispersed and consolidated. See ATP 3-37.10 for the strengths and weaknesses of each approach.)

4-95. Troop movements and resupply convoys are critical. Staffs balance terrain management, movement planning, convoy security requirements, and traffic-circulation control priorities. They plan multiple routes

Chapter 4

throughout an AO and closely control their use. Commanders may allocate mobility resources to maintain main supply routes to support units and supplies moving forward and to evacuate personnel and equipment to the rear. Commanders coordinate movements with affected organic and external Army aviation, fire support, air defense units, and ground maneuver units. As required, military police protect movements, prevent congestion, and respond to maneuver plan changes. Military police can provide necessary convoy escorts, or maneuver units can use their resources, to provide necessary convoy security. In some circumstances transportation units can provide their own security.

Survivability Operations

4-96. An attacking enemy force usually has the initiative. A defending commander must take a wide range of actions to reduce the risk of losses, including developing a survivability plan. Survivability in the defense prioritizes hardening command posts, artillery positions, air and missile defenses, and other critical equipment and supply areas. It also includes preparing individual, crew-served, and combat vehicle fighting positions.

4-97. To avoid detection and destruction by enemy forces, units move frequently and quickly establish survivability positions. To provide flexibility, units may need primary, alternate, and supplementary positions. This is particularly true of units defending key or decisive terrain. Units enhance their survivability using concealment, military deception, decoy or dummy positions, dispersion, and field fortifications. Commanders increase security during defensive preparations because an enemy force will attack lightly defended areas whenever possible.

4-98. When preparing area and mobile defenses, engineer units assist maneuver and supporting units prepare survivability positions. Commanders locate these positions throughout a defending unit's security area, MBA, and support area. Requirements beyond the capabilities of BCT engineer battalions pass through a higher headquarters to an attached Army maneuver enhancement brigade or any functional engineer brigade supporting the division or corps. These engineer units also prepare any strong points required by the division or corps concept of operations.

4-99. Survivability tasks include using engineer equipment to help in constructing trenches, command post shelters, and artillery, firing, radar, and combat vehicle fighting positions. Commanders provide guidance on the level of protection (such as hull defilade, turret defilade, or overhead cover), system priorities, and early employment of specialized engineer equipment that can construct survivability positions. (See ATP 3-37.34 for additional information concerning the construction and maintenance of survivability positions.)

4-100. Commanders use dispersion to limit the damage done by enemy attacks. Enemy forces should never be able to put a unit out of action with just a single attack. Dispersed troops and vehicles force attacking forces to concentrate on a single small target that may be missed. The wider the dispersion of unit personnel and equipment is, the greater potential for limiting damage it has. Commanders position forces and installations to avoid congestion, but they do not disperse them to the extent that there is a risk of defeat in detail by an enemy employing conventional munitions or weapons of mass destruction.

4-101. Commanders protect supply stocks against blast, shrapnel, incendiaries, and CBRN contamination using dispersion and constructing survivability positions. Forces can protect vehicles carrying supplies against almost anything but a direct hit by constructing berms large enough to accommodate the vehicles and deep enough to keep supplies below ground level. The echelon staff advises sustainment operators about storage area site selection that reduces the requirements for engineer survivability support without reducing the required degree of protection.

4-102. Units also use cover to limit the amount of damage and casualties that they can receive because of an enemy attack. Folds in the earth, natural depressions, trees, buildings, and walls offer cover. If a commander deploys in flat terrain lacking cover, digging in or sandbagging can offer some protection. Units employ obscuration if they are moving and cannot use natural cover or cannot build fortifications.

Chemical, Biological, Radiological, and Nuclear Defense

4-103. Defending units are often in fixed positions and have an increased vulnerability to CBRN threats and hazards. Commanders specify the degree of acceptable risk and establish priorities for CBRN defense assets.

4-104. Units establish, train, rehearse, and exercise a CBRN defense plan to protect personnel and equipment from CBRN hazards. Mission-oriented protective posture (known as MOPP) analysis can be used as a tool to support—

- Determining the appropriate protective posture, estimating unit and personnel effectiveness (for example, mission degradation).
- Estimating additional logistic requirements (for example, water resupply and individual protective equipment replenishment).
- Assessing and weighing the tradeoffs between agent exposures versus degraded performance (for example, wearing full CBRN protective equipment).

Medical personnel continuously maintain and conduct comprehensive health surveillance (health, medical, occupational, and environmental health surveillance). Commanders ensure that their units can conduct operational and thorough decontamination of military personnel and equipment. Commanders are responsible for CBRN passive defense training to prepare their units to respond properly to CBRN threats.

4-105. Commanders integrate CBRN reconnaissance and surveillance into the overall information collection plan. Employment of CBRN reconnaissance and surveillance capabilities should not duplicate the efforts of conventional reconnaissance assets.

4-106. CBRN personnel contribute to the overall protection of units located in defensive positions. CBRN personnel perform CBRN vulnerability assessments including a threat assessment and vulnerability analysis, and they recommend vulnerability reduction measures for commanders to consider before and after units move into their defensive positions. These assessments provide a list of preventive measures that can range from the use of obscurants, reconnaissance, mission-oriented protective posture, and other aspects of CBRN defense. (For more information on CBRN vulnerability assessment, see ATP 3-11.36. For more information on CBRN protection, see ATP 3-11.32.)

Physical Security and Antiterrorism

4-107. Enemy forces employ all means to attack defending maneuver elements, command and communications nodes, LOCs, sustainment sites, and civilian population centers in an attempt to disrupt the defense. Commanders pay attention to physical security and antiterrorism operations throughout a defense. This is especially true when a defending unit conducts noncontiguous operations.

4-108. The success of a unit defense may depend on protecting the support area from enemy attacks. Commanders must address the early detection and immediate destruction of enemy forces attempting to attack support areas. Enemy attacks in these areas against sustainment and other facilities can range in size from individual saboteurs to enemy airborne or air assault insertions targeted against key military and civilian facilities and capabilities. These enemy activities, especially at smaller unit levels, may even precede the onset of large-scale combat and be almost indistinguishable from terrorist acts.

4-109. Planners determine how military police elements supporting a defending unit will enhance unit physical security and antiterrorism capabilities by performing area security tasks inside and outside an echelon support area. Military police may defeat Level II threats against bases and base clusters located in an echelon support area. They will maintain contact with Level III threats until a tactical combat force can respond. (See ATP 3-91 for a discussion of the threat levels. See FM 3-90-2 for a discussion of security operations.)

Conduct Population and Resource Control

4-110. Commanders plan for dislocated civilians and the effect that they have on the defense. Civil affairs units help commanders in planning population and resource control measures. A defending unit uses host-nation and international organizations as much as possible to minimize the effects of disaster or conflict on dislocated civilians and thereby avoid diverting unit resources to conduct stability operations.

Chapter 4

BREAKOUT

4-111. **A *breakout* is an operation conducted by an encircled force to regain freedom of movement or contact with friendly units.** A breakout differs from other attacks only in that a simultaneous defense in other areas of the perimeter must be maintained. An encircled force normally attempts to conduct a breakout when—
- Opportunity exists to attack.
- An encircled force does not have sufficient relative combat power to defend itself against enemy forces attempting the encirclement.
- An encircled force does not have adequate terrain available to conduct its defense.
- An encircled force cannot sustain itself long enough to be relieved by forces outside the encirclement.

EXFILTRATION

4-112. If the success of a breakout attack appears questionable, or if it fails and a relief operation is not planned, one way to preserve a portion of the force is through organized exfiltration. (See FM 3-90-1 for a detailed description of exfiltration.)

ATTACKING DEEPER INTO ENEMY TERRITORY

4-113. A COA that enemy forces do not expect from an encircled force is to attack deeper to seize key terrain. It involves great risk, but it may offer the only feasible COA under some circumstances. Attacking may allow an encircled unit to move to a location where it can be extracted by other ground, naval, or air forces. Attacking deeper is only feasible if a unit can sustain itself while isolated, although sustainment can come from aerial resupply and enemy supply stocks.

4-114. When an enemy is attacking, an encircled friendly force that attacks deeper into the enemy rear area may disrupt the enemy's offense and provide an opportunity for linkup from another direction. If an enemy is defending and the attacking force finds itself isolated, it may continue the attack toward its assigned objective or a new objective located on more favorable defensive terrain.

LINKUP

4-115. **A *linkup* is a meeting of friendly ground forces, which occurs in a variety of circumstances.** It happens when an advancing force reaches an objective previously seized by an airborne or air assault forces. A linkup can also occur when an encircled element breaks out to rejoin friendly forces or a force comes to the relief of an encircled force. It also occurs when converging maneuver forces meet by moving toward each other, or when one force is stationary. Whenever possible, joining forces exchange as much information as possible before starting a linkup operation. The headquarters ordering the linkup establishes—
- The common operational picture.
- The command and support relationship and responsibilities of each force before, during, and after linkup.
- FSCMs and direct fire control measures.
- The linkup method.
- Recognition signals and communication procedures.
- Subsequent operations.

TRANSITION

4-116. Defending commanders assess the success of their defense and determine if they can transition to the offense. If a defense is unsuccessful, defending commanders transition into retrograde operations. Transition from one type of operation to another requires mental as well as physical agility from the involved formations and an accurate understanding of the situation.

4-117. Commanders deliberately plan for the transition process and allow the setting of the conditions necessary for a successful transition. Such planning addresses the need to control the tempo of operations, maintain contact with both enemy and friendly forces, and keep enemy forces off balance. It establishes the procedures and priorities by which a unit prepares for its next mission. It establishes the required organization of forces and control measures necessary for success in accordance with the mission variables.

4-118. Prior planning decreases the time needed to adjust the tempo of combat operations when a unit transitions from defensive operations to offensive operations. This planning allowing subordinate units to conduct parallel planning and prepare for subsequent operations. Preparations include resupplying unit basic loads and repositioning or reallocating supporting systems.

4-119. Planning also reduces the amount of time and confusion that arises when a unit is unsuccessful in its defensive efforts and must transition to retrograde operations. Commanders designate units to conduct denial operations and to evacuate casualties and equipment. Commanders use retrograde operations to preserve their forces as combat-capable formations until they can establish those conditions necessary for a successful defense. Plans should account for both failure and success, and they should account for a transition to offensive or stability operations.

TRANSITION TO THE OFFENSE

4-120. A defending commander seeks a window of opportunity to transition to offensive operations by anticipating when and where an enemy force will reach its culminating point or require an operational pause before it can continue. During these windows, the combat power ratios mostly favor a defending force. An enemy force will do everything it can to keep a friendly force from knowing when it is overextended. The following items indicate that an enemy force is becoming overextended:
- Enemy forces begin to transition to the defense—this defense may be by forces in or out of contact with friendly forces.
- Enemy forces suffer heavy losses.
- Enemy forces start to deploy before encountering friendly forces.
- Enemy forces are defeated in most engagements.
- Enemy forces are committed piecemeal in continued attacks.
- Enemy aviation forces are used in place of ineffective ground forces.
- Enemy reserve forces are identified among attacking forces.
- Examination of captured or killed enemy soldiers and captured or destroyed enemy equipment and supplies shows that the enemy forces cannot adequately sustain themselves.
- Enemy forces have a noticeable reduction in their tempo of operations.
- Local counterattacks meet with unexpected success.

4-121. In a mobile defense, transitioning to an offense generally follows a striking force's attack. In an area defense, commanders designate a portion of their force to conduct the counterattack, selecting units based on the commander's concept of operations. However, commanders allocate available reserves to this counterattack effort.

4-122. Commanders reorganize and resupply to support the offense. These actions require a transition in the sustainment effort, with a shift in emphasis from ensuring a capability to defend from a chosen location to an emphasis on ensuring a force's ability to advance and maneuver. For example, in a defense the sustainment effort may have focused on the forward stockage of Class IV and V items and the rapid evacuation of damaged systems. In an offense, the sustainment effort may need to focus on providing petroleum, oils, and lubricants; forward repair and maintenance; and replacement of combat losses. A transition is often a time in which units can perform deferred equipment maintenance. Additional assets may also be available on a temporary basis for casualty evacuation and medical treatment because of a reduction in the tempo of operations.

4-123. Commanders should not wait too long to transition from defensive operations to offensive operations as an enemy force approaches its culminating point. Enemy forces will be dispersed, extended in depth, and weakened. At that time, any enemy defensive preparations will be hasty, and enemy forces will not be adequately prepared for defense. Commanders want enemy forces weakened when transitioning to the offense, and they do not want to give an enemy force time to prepare for the defense. Additionally, the psychological shock on enemy soldiers will be greater if they suddenly find themselves defending on unfavorable terms.

4-124. There are two methods for transitioning to an offense. The first, and generally preferred method, is to attack using forces not previously committed to a defense. This method is preferred because defending units may still be decisively engaged, tired, or depleted. These attacking forces may come from the reserve or consist of reinforcements. Since these forces have not recently been actively involved in combat, they are more likely to—

- Be at authorized strength levels.
- Have a higher combat system operationally readiness rate.
- Have leaders and Soldiers who are more likely to be rested and more capable of prolonged, continuous operations.
- Have a complete basic load of supplies.
- Have the time and energy to plan and prepare to conduct the offensive operations.
- Be able to maneuver out of physical contact with an enemy force.

4-125. The second method is to perform a type of offensive operation using currently defending forces. This method generally has the advantage of being more rapidly executed and thus more likely to catch an enemy force by surprise. Speed of execution in this method results from not having to conduct an approach or tactical road march from reserve assembly areas or, in the case of reinforcements, move from other AOs and reception, staging, onward movement, and integration locations. Speed also results from not having to conduct a forward passage of lines and performing the liaison necessary to establish a common operational picture that includes knowledge of the enemy force's patterns of operation.

4-126. If units in contact participate in an attack, commanders must retain sufficient forces in contact to fix enemy forces. Commanders concentrate an attack by reinforcing select subordinate units so they can execute the attack and, if necessary, maintain the existing defense. Commanders can also adjust the defensive boundaries of subordinate units so entire units can withdraw and concentrate for an attack.

TRANSITION TO STABILITY

4-127. A force may transition from defensive operations to stability operations. This generally occurs if the force reaches and establishes a defense along a LOA. Then, there may be a negotiated end to hostilities from which the force transitions to stability. While improving its defensive preparations, the force may begin to increase the amount of resources dedicated to stability.

Chapter 5
Enabling Operations

The enabling operations discussed in this chapter are reconnaissance, security, troop movement, relief in place, and passage of lines. Enabling operations apply to all elements of decisive action. Other publications discuss other enabling operations. For example, FM 3-13 discusses information operations, ATP 3-90.4 discusses mobility operations, and ATP 3-90.8 discusses countermobility operations. Commanders direct enabling operations to support the conduct of the offensive, defensive, and stability operations and defense support of civil authorities tasks. Enabling operations are usually conducted by commanders as part of their shaping operations or supporting efforts.

RECONNAISSANCE

5-1. *Reconnaissance* is a mission undertaken to obtain, by visual observation or other detection methods, information about the activities and resources of an enemy or adversary, or to secure data concerning the meteorological, hydrographic, or geographic characteristics of a particular area (JP 2-0). Reconnaissance accomplished by small units primarily relies on the human dynamic rather than technical means. Reconnaissance is a focused collection effort. Units perform it before, during, and after operations to provide commanders and staffs information used in the IPB process so they can formulate, confirm, or modify COAs.

5-2. Commanders orient their reconnaissance assets by identifying a reconnaissance objective within an AO. **The *reconnaissance objective* is a terrain feature, geographic area, enemy force, adversary, or other mission or operational variable about which the commander wants to obtain additional information.** Every reconnaissance mission specifies a reconnaissance objective that clarifies the intent of the effort and prioritizes those efforts by specifying the most important information to obtain. Commanders assign reconnaissance objectives based on priority information requirements resulting from the IPB process and the reconnaissance asset's capabilities and limitations. As information about a specific location, such as the cross country trafficability of a specific area, a reconnaissance objective can confirm a specific activity or location of a threat. Furthermore, a reconnaissance unit uses the reconnaissance objective to guide it in setting priorities when it lacks time to complete all the tasks associated with a specific type of reconnaissance operation.

5-3. There are seven fundamentals of successful reconnaissance. Commanders—
- Ensure continuous reconnaissance.
- Do not keep reconnaissance assets in reserve.
- Orient on reconnaissance objectives.
- Report information rapidly and accurately.
- Retain freedom of maneuver.
- Gain and maintain enemy contact.
- Develop the situation rapidly.

5-4. The responsibility for accomplishing reconnaissance does not reside solely with reconnaissance units. Every unit has an implied mission to report information about the terrain, civilian activities, and friendly and enemy dispositions. Troops in contact with an enemy and reconnaissance patrols of maneuver units, at all echelons, collect information on enemy units and activities. In echelon support and consolidation areas, reserve maneuver forces, functional and multifunctional support and sustainment elements, other governmental agencies, and multinational forces observe and report civilian, adversary, and enemy activity

Chapter 5

and significant changes in terrain trafficability. Although all units conduct reconnaissance, ground cavalry, aviation attack reconnaissance units, scouts, and special forces are specifically trained to conduct reconnaissance operations. Some branches, such as the Corps of Engineers and Chemical Corps, conduct specific reconnaissance operations that complement the force's overall reconnaissance effort. However, BCT, division, and corps commanders primarily use their organic or attached reconnaissance—ground or air—and intelligence elements to accomplish reconnaissance.

5-5. The five types of reconnaissance operations are—

- *Area reconnaissance* **is a type of reconnaissance operation that focuses on obtaining detailed information about the terrain or enemy activity within a prescribed area**. Commanders assign an area reconnaissance when information on the enemy situation is limited or when focused reconnaissance will yield specific information on the area in question. An area reconnaissance differs from a zone reconnaissance in that the unit conducting an area reconnaissance starts from an LD.
- **A** *reconnaissance in force* **is a type of reconnaissance operation designed to discover or test the enemy's strength, dispositions, and reactions or to obtain other information**. A commander assigns a reconnaissance in force when an enemy force is operating within an area and the commander cannot obtain adequate intelligence by other means. The unit commander plans for both the retrograde or reinforcement of the friendly force (in case it encounters superior enemy forces) and for the exploitation of its success.
- *Route reconnaissance* **is a type of reconnaissance operation to obtain detailed information of a specified route and all terrain from which the enemy could influence movement along that route**. Route reconnaissance provides new or updated information on route conditions, such as obstacles and bridge classifications, and enemy, adversary, and civilian activity along the route.
- *Special reconnaissance* is reconnaissance and surveillance actions conducted as a special operation in hostile, denied, or diplomatically and/or politically sensitive environments to collect or verify information of strategic or operational significance, employing military capabilities not normally found in conventional forces (JP 3-05). Special reconnaissance provides an additional capability for commanders and supplements other conventional reconnaissance and surveillance actions.
- *Zone reconnaissance* **is a type of reconnaissance operation that involves a directed effort to obtain detailed information on all routes, obstacles, terrain, and enemy forces within a zone defined by boundaries**. Obstacles include existing, reinforcing, and areas with CBRN contamination. Commanders assign a zone reconnaissance mission when they need additional information on a zone before committing other forces. Zone reconnaissance is the most time- and resource-intensive form of reconnaissance.

SECURITY OPERATIONS

5-6. The main difference between conducting security operations and reconnaissance is that security operations orient on the force or facility being protected while reconnaissance orients on the enemy and terrain. Security operations aim to protect a force from surprise and reduce the unknowns in any situation. Commanders conduct security operations to the front, flanks, or rear of a friendly force. Security operations are shaping operations. As a shaping operation, economy of force is often a consideration when planning.

5-7. The four types of security operations are—

- *Area security* **is a type of security operation conducted to protect friendly forces, lines of communications, and activities within a specific area**. The security force may be protecting the civilian population, civil institutions, and civilian infrastructure with the unit's AO.
- *Cover* **is a type of security operation done independent of the main body to protect them by fighting to gain time while preventing enemy ground observation of and direct fire against the main body**. Commanders use the cover task offensively and defensively. (Cover as a doctrinal term also has other definitions.)

- ***Guard* is a type of security operation done to protect the main body by fighting to gain time while preventing enemy ground observation of and direct fire against the main body**. Units performing a guard cannot operate independently. They rely upon fires, functional support, and multifunctional support assets of the main body.
- ***Screen* is a type of security operation that primarily provides early warning to the protected force**.

5-8. The cover, guard, and screen security operations employ increasing levels of combat power and provide increasing levels of security for a force's main body. However, more combat power in the security force means less combat power for the main body. Area security preserves a commander's freedom to move reserves, position fire support means, provide for command and control, and conduct sustaining operations.

5-9. All maneuver forces can conduct security operations. All three types of Army BCTs—armored, infantry, and Stryker—conduct security operations as part of their mission-essential task lists. Commanders ensure that subordinate units conduct security operations required by the situation. Habitual support relationships with attachments and standard operating procedures are required to obtain proficiency in the conduct of these operations.

5-10. Successful security operations depend on properly applying five fundamentals:
- Provide early and accurate warning.
- Provide reaction time and maneuver space.
- Orient on the force, area, or facility.
- Perform continuous reconnaissance.
- Maintain enemy contact.

(See FM 3-90-2 and FM 3-98 for additional information on the conduct of security operations.)

TROOP MOVEMENT

5-11. ***Troop movement* is the movement of Soldiers and units from one place to another by any available means**. The ability of a commander to posture friendly forces for a decisive or shaping operation depends on the commander's ability to move those forces. The essence of battlefield agility is the capability to conduct rapid and orderly movement to concentrate combat power at decisive points and times. Successful movement places troops and equipment at their destination at the proper time, ready for combat. The following are types of troop movements:
- ***Administrative movement* is a movement in which troops and vehicles are arranged to expedite their movement and conserve time and energy when no enemy ground interference is anticipated**. Commanders only conduct administrative movements in secure areas. Commanders normally do not employ administrative movements once their units deploy into combat operations. The echelon logistic staff officer usually supervises these types of moves. (See FM 4-01 for a discussion of Army transportation operations.)
- ***Approach march* is the advance of a combat unit when direct contact with the enemy is intended**. An approach march emphasizes speed over tactical deployment. Armored, Stryker, and infantry forces conduct tactical road marches and approach marches.
- **A *tactical road march* is a rapid movement used to relocate units within an area of operations to prepare for combat operations**. The primary use of a tactical road march is rapid movement. However, the moving force employs security measures even when contact with enemy forces is not expected. During tactical road marches, commanders are always prepared to take immediate action if an enemy attacks. (See ATP 4-01.45 for a discussion of tactical convoy operations.)

METHODS OF TROOP MOVEMENT

5-12. Troop movements are made by dismounted marches and mounted marches using vehicles. Units also use available transportation modes—motor transport, air, rail, and water—in various combinations. The method employed depends on the situation, size, and composition of the moving unit; distance the unit must cover; urgency of execution; and condition of the troops. It also depends on the availability, suitability, and capacity of the different means of transportation. Troop movements over extended distances have significant

Chapter 5

sustainment requirements. When necessary, dismounted and mounted marches can be hurried by conducting a forced march. (See FM 4-01 for a discussion of these various transportation modes.)

MOVEMENT CONTROL

5-13. Movement control is the dual process of committing allocated transportation assets and regulating movements according to command priorities to synchronize distribution flow over lines of communications to sustain land forces. Commanders' priorities guide the conduct of movement control. Movement control gives commanders the ability to deconflict troop movements with the distribution of supplies and services.

RELIEF IN PLACE

5-14. A *relief in place* is an operation in which, by direction of higher authority, all or part of a unit is replaced in an area by the incoming unit and the responsibilities of the replaced elements for the mission and the assigned zone of operations are transferred to the incoming unit (JP 3-07.3). (*Note*. The Army uses an AO instead of a zone of operations.) The incoming unit continues the operation as ordered. Commanders conduct a relief in place as part of a larger operation, primarily to maintain the combat effectiveness of committed units. The higher echelon headquarters directs when and where to conduct a relief, and it establishes the appropriate control measures. The commanders participating in the relief in place communicate when the relieving commander has sufficient combat power and understanding of the AO to assume responsibility of the area.

5-15. There are three types of relief in place operations:
- A *sequential relief in place* **occurs when each element within the relieved unit is relieved in succession, from right to left or left to right, depending on how it is deployed.**
- A *simultaneous relief in place* **occurs when all elements are relieved at the same time.**
- A *staggered relief in place* **occurs when a commander relieves each element in a sequence determined by the tactical situation, not its geographical orientation.**

5-16. Simultaneous relief in place takes the least time to execute but is easily detected by the enemy. Sequential or staggered reliefs can occur over a significant amount of time. These three relief techniques can occur regardless of the mission and operational environment in which the unit is participating.

5-17. A relief in place can be characterized as either deliberate or hasty depending on the amount of planning and preparation associated with the relief. The major differences are the depth and detail of planning and the time available. Deliberate planning allows unit commanders and staffs to identify, develop, and coordinate solutions to potential problems before they occur. (See FM 3-90-2 for additional information on the conduct of a relief in place.)

PASSAGE OF LINES

5-18. A *passage of lines* is an operation in which a force moves forward or rearward through another force's combat positions with the intention of moving into or out of contact with the enemy (JP 3-18). A passage of lines may be designated as a forward or rearward passage of lines. A passage of lines occurs under two conditions:
- A *forward passage of lines* **occurs when a unit passes through another unit's positions while moving toward the enemy.**
- A *rearward passage of lines* **occurs when a unit passes through another unit's positions while moving away from the enemy.**

Ideally, a passage of lines does not interfere with conducting the stationary unit's operations. (See FM 3-90-2 for additional information on passage of lines.)

5-19. A commander conducts a passage of lines to continue an attack or conduct a counterattack, retrograde, or security operation when one unit cannot bypass another unit's position. The conduct of a passage of lines potentially involves close combat. It involves transferring the responsibility for an AO between two commanders. That transfer of authority usually occurs when roughly two-thirds of the passing force has moved through the passage point. If not directed by higher authority, the two unit commanders determine—

by mutual agreement—the time to transfer command. They disseminate this information to the lowest levels of both organizations.

5-20. A commander's reasons for conducting a passage of lines are to—
- Sustain the tempo of the offense.
- Maintain the viability of the defense by transferring responsibility from one unit to another.
- Transition from a delay or security operation by one force to a defense.
- Free a unit for another mission or task.

The headquarters directing the passage of lines is responsible for determining when the passage of lines starts and finishes.

This page intentionally left blank.

Glossary

The glossary lists acronyms and terms with Army or joint definitions. Where Army and joint definitions differ, (Army) precedes the definition. Terms for which ADP 3-90 is the proponent are marked with an asterisk (*). The proponent publication for other terms is listed in parentheses after the definition.

SECTION I – ACRONYMS AND ABBREVIATIONS

ADP	Army doctrine publication
AO	area of operations
ATP	Army techniques publication
BCT	brigade combat team
COA	course of action
DA	Department of the Army
FEBA	forward edge of the battle area
FLOT	forward line of own troops
FM	field manual
FPF	final protective fire
FSCM	fire support coordination measure
IPB	intelligence preparation of the battlefield
JAGIC	joint air-ground integration center
JP	joint publication
LD	line of departure
LOA	limit of advance
LOC	line of communications
MBA	main battle area
TTP	tactics, techniques, and procedures
U.S.	United States

SECTION II – TERMS

*actions on contact

A series of combat actions, often conducted nearly simultaneously, taken on contact with the enemy to develop the situation.

*administrative movement

A movement in which troops and vehicles are arranged to expedite their movement and conserve time and energy when no enemy ground interference is anticipated.

airspace control

Capabilities and procedures used to increase operational effectiveness by promoting the safe, efficient, and flexible use of airspace. (JP 3-52)

*alternate position
> A defensive position that the commander assigns to a unit or weapon system for occupation when the primary position becomes untenable or unsuitable for carrying out the assigned task.

*approach march
> The advance of a combat unit when direct contact with the enemy is intended.

*area defense
> A type of defensive operation that concentrates on denying enemy forces access to designated terrain for a specific time rather than destroying the enemy outright.

area of influence
> A geographical area wherein a commander is directly capable of influencing operations by maneuver or fire support systems normally under the commander's command or control. (JP 3-0)

area of interest
> That area of concern to the commander, including the area of influence, areas adjacent thereto, and extending into enemy territory. (JP 3-0)

area of operations
> An operational area defined by a commander for land and maritime forces that should be large enough to accomplish their missions and protect their forces. (JP 3-0)

*area reconnaissance
> A type of reconnaissance operation that focuses on obtaining detailed information about the terrain or enemy activity within a prescribed area.

*area security
> A type of security operation conducted to protect friendly forces, lines of communications, and activities within a specific area.

ARFOR
> The Army component and senior Army headquarters of all Army forces assigned or attached to a combatant command, subordinate joint force command, joint functional command, or multinational command. (FM 3-94)

Army personnel recovery
> The military efforts taken to prepare for and execute the recovery and reintegration of isolated personnel. (FM 3-50)

*art of tactics
> Three interrelated aspects: the creative and flexible array of means to accomplish missions, decision making under conditions of uncertainty when faced with a thinking and adaptive enemy, and the understanding of the effects of combat on Soldiers.

*assailable flank
> A flank exposed to attack or envelopment.

*assault position
> A covered and concealed position short of the objective from which final preparations are made to assault the objective.

*assault time
> The moment to attack the initial objectives throughout the geographical scope of the operation.

assured mobility
> A framework—of processes, actions, and capabilities—that assures the ability of a force to deploy, move, and maneuver where and when desired, to achieve the commander's intent. (ATP 3-90.4)

*attack
> A type of offensive operation that destroys or defeats enemy forces, seizes and secures terrain, or both.

*attack by fire position
    The general position from which a unit performs the tactical task of attack by fire.

*attack position
    (Army) The last position an attacking force occupies or passes through before crossing the line of departure.

*avenue of approach
    (Army) A path used by an attacking force leading to its objective or to key terrain. Avenues of approach exist in all domains.

*axis of advance
    The general area through which the bulk of a unit's combat power must move.

basic load
    The quantity of supplies required to be on hand within, and moved by a unit or formation, expressed according to the wartime organization of the unit or formation and maintained at the prescribed levels. (JP 4-09)

*battalion
    A unit consisting of two or more company-, battery-, or troop-size units and a headquarters.

*battalion task force
    A maneuver battalion-size unit consisting of a battalion headquarters, at least one assigned company size-element, and at least one attached company-size element from another maneuver or support unit (functional or multifunctional).

*battery
    A company-size unit in a field artillery or air defense artillery battalion.

*battle
    A set of related engagements that lasts longer and involves larger forces than an engagement.

*battle drill
    Rehearsed and well understood actions made in response to common battlefield occurrences.

*battle handover line
    A designated phase line where responsibility transitions from the stationary force to the moving force and vice versa.

*battle position
    A defensive location oriented on a likely enemy avenue of approach.

*breakout
    An operation conducted by an encircled force to regain freedom of movement or contact with friendly units.

*brigade
    A unit consisting of two or more battalions and a headquarters company or detachment.

*brigade combat team
    (Army) A combined arms organization consisting of a brigade headquarters, at least two maneuver battalions, and necessary supporting functional capabilities.

*bypass criteria
    Measures established by higher echelon headquarters that specify the conditions and size under which enemy units and contact may be avoided.

civil-military operations

Activities of a commander performed by designated military forces that establish, maintain, influence, or exploit relations between military forces and indigenous populations and institutions by directly supporting the achievement of objectives relating to the reestablishment or maintenance of stability within a region or host nation. (JP 3-57)

clearance of fires

The process by which the supported commander ensures that fires or their effects will have no unintended consequences on friendly units or the scheme of maneuver. (FM 3-09)

close combat

Warfare carried out on land in a direct-fire fight, supported by direct and indirect fires and other assets. (ADP 3-0)

combat information

Unevaluated data, gathered by or provided directly to the tactical commander which, due to its highly perishable nature or the criticality of the situation, cannot be processed into tactical intelligence in time to satisfy the user's tactical intelligence requirements. (JP 2-01)

combat power

(Army) The total means of destructive, constructive, and information capabilities that a military unit or formation can apply at a given time. (ADP 3-0).

combined arms

The synchronized and simultaneous application of arms to achieve an effect greater than if each element was used separately or sequentially. (ADP 3-0)

command and control warfighting function

The related tasks and a system that enable commanders to synchronize and converge all elements of combat power. (ADP 3-0)

*committed force

A force in contact with an enemy or deployed on a specific mission or course of action, which precludes its employment elsewhere.

*company

A unit consisting of two or more platoons, usually of the same type, with a headquarters and a limited capacity for self-support.

*company team

A combined arms organization formed by attaching one or more nonorganic armor, mechanized infantry, Stryker infantry, or infantry platoons to a tank, mechanized infantry, Stryker, or infantry company, either in exchange for, or in addition to, its organic platoons.

concept of operations

(Army) A statement that directs the manner in which subordinate units cooperate to accomplish the mission and establishes the sequence of actions the force will use to achieve the end state. (ADP 5-0)

consolidate gains

Activities to make enduring any temporary operational success and to set the conditions for a sustainable security environment, allowing for a transition of control to legitimate authorities. (ADP 3-0)

coordinating altitude

An airspace coordinating measure that uses altitude to separate users and as the transition between different airspace control elements. (JP 3-52)

coordination level

A procedural method to separate fixed- and rotary-wing aircraft by determining an altitude below which fixed-wing aircraft normally will not fly. (JP 3-52)

*corps
    An echelon of command and tactical formation that employs divisions, multi-functional brigades, and functional brigades to achieve objectives on land.

countermobility operations
    (Army) Those combined arms activities that use or enhance the effects of natural and man-made obstacles to deny enemy freedom of movement and maneuver. (ATP 3-90.8)

*cover
    (Army) A type of security operation done independent of the main body to protect them by fighting to gain time while preventing enemy ground observation of and direct fire against the main body.

*crew
    A small military unit that consists of all personnel operating a particular system.

decisive operation
    The operation that directly accomplishes the mission. (ADP 3-0)

*decisive terrain
    Key terrain whose seizure and retention is mandatory for successful mission accomplishment.

*decisive engagement
    An engagement in which a unit is considered fully committed and cannot maneuver or extricate itself.

defeat
    To render a force incapable of achieving its objectives. (ADP 3-0)

*defeat in detail
    Concentrating overwhelming combat power against separate parts of a force rather than defeating the entire force at once.

defeat mechanism
    A method through which friendly forces accomplish their mission against enemy opposition. (ADP 3-0)

defensive operation
    An operation to defeat an enemy attack, gain time, economize forces, and develop conditions favorable for offensive or stability operations. (ADP 3-0)

*delay
    When a force under pressure trades space for time by slowing down the enemy's momentum and inflicting maximum damage on enemy forces without becoming decisively engaged.

*deliberate operation
    An operation in which the tactical situation allows the development and coordination of detailed plans, including multiple branches and sequels.

*detachment
    A tactical element organized on either a temporary or permanent basis for special duties.

*direction of attack
    A specific direction or assigned route a force uses and does not deviate from when attacking.

*disengagement line
    A phase line located on identifiable terrain that, when crossed by the enemy, signals to defending elements that it is time to displace to their next position.

*division
    An echelon of command and tactical formation that employs brigade combat teams, multi-functional brigades, and functional brigades to achieve objectives on land.

economy of force
> The judicious employment and distribution of forces so as to expend the minimum essential combat power on secondary efforts to allocate the maximum possible combat power on primary efforts. (JP 3-0)

*encirclement operations
> Operations where one force loses its freedom of maneuver because an opposing force is able to isolate it by controlling all ground lines of communications and reinforcement.

engagement
> A tactical conflict, usually between opposing lower echelon maneuver forces. (JP 3-0)

*engagement area
> An area where the commander intends to contain and destroy an enemy force with the massed effects of all available weapons and supporting systems.

*exploitation
> (Army) A type of offensive operation that usually follows a successful attack and is designed to disorganize the enemy in depth.

*field army
> An echelon of command that employs multiple corps, divisions, multi-functional brigades, and functional brigades to achieve objectives on land.

*final coordination line
> A phase line close to the enemy position used to coordinate the lifting or shifting of supporting fires with the final deployment of maneuver elements.

final protective fire
> An immediately available, prearranged barrier of fire designed to impede enemy movement across defensive lines or areas. (JP 3-09.3)

fire support coordination measure
> A measure employed by commanders to facilitate the rapid engagement of targets and simultaneously provide safeguards for friendly forces. (JP 3-0).

fires warfighting function
> The related tasks and systems that create and converge effects in all domains against the adversary or enemy to enable operations across the range of military operations. (ADP 3-0)

*fire team
> A small military unit typically containing four or fewer Soldiers.

*fixing force
> A force designated to supplement the striking force by preventing the enemy from moving from a specific area for a specific time.

*flank
> The right or left limit of a unit.

*flanking position
> A geographical location on the flank of a force from which effective fires can be placed on that flank.

*forms of maneuver
> Distinct tactical combinations of fire and movement with a unique set of doctrinal characteristics that differ primarily in the relationship between the maneuvering force and the enemy.

forward edge of the battle area
> The foremost limits of a series of areas in which ground combat units are deployed to coordinate fire support, the positioning of forces, or the maneuver of units, excluding areas in which covering or screening forces are operating. (JP 3-09.3)

forward line of own troops

A line that indicates the most forward positions of friendly forces in any kind of military operation at a specific time. (JP 3-03)

*forward passage of lines

Occurs when a unit passes through another unit's positions while moving toward the enemy.

*guard

A type of security operation done to protect the main body by fighting to gain time while preventing enemy ground observation of and direct fire against the main body.

*hasty operation

An operation in which a commander directs immediately available forces, using fragmentary orders, to perform tasks with minimal preparation, trading planning and preparation time for speed of execution.

intelligence operations

(Army) The tasks undertaken by military intelligence units through the intelligence disciplines to obtain information to satisfy validated requirements. (ADP 2-0)

intelligence warfighting function

The related tasks and systems that facilitate understanding the enemy, terrain, weather, civil considerations, and other significant aspects of the operational environment. (ADP 3-0)

*key terrain

(Army) An identifiable characteristic whose seizure or retention affords a marked advantage to either combatant.

*limit of advance

A phase line used to control forward progress of the attack.

*line of contact

A general trace delineating the location where friendly and enemy forces are engaged.

line of departure

In land warfare, a line designated to coordinate the departure of attack elements. (JP 3-31)

*linkup

A meeting of friendly ground forces, which occurs in a variety of circumstances.

*local security

The low-level security activities conducted near a unit to prevent surprise by the enemy.

*main battle area

The area where the commander intends to deploy the bulk of the unit's combat power and conduct decisive operations to defeat an attacking enemy.

*main body

The principal part of a tactical command or formation. It does not include detached elements of the command, such as advance guards, flank guards, and covering forces.

*maneuver

(Army) Movement in conjunction with fires. (joint) Employment of forces in the operational area, through movement in combination with fires and information, to achieve a position of advantage in respect to the enemy. (JP 3-0)

*meeting engagement

A combat action that occurs when a moving force, incompletely deployed for battle, engages an enemy at an unexpected time and place.

*mobile defense

A type of defensive operation that concentrates on the destruction or defeat of the enemy through a decisive attack by a striking force.

mobility tasks

Those combined arms activities that mitigate the effects of obstacles to enable freedom of movement and maneuver. (ATP 3-90.4)

movement and maneuver warfighting function

The related tasks and systems that move and employ forces to achieve a position of relative advantage over the enemy and other threats. (ADP 3-0)

*movement

The positioning of combat power to establish the conditions for maneuver.

movement control

(Army) The dual process of committing allocated transportation assets and regulating movements according to command priorities to synchronize distribution flow over lines of communications to sustain land forces. (ADP 4-0)

*movement formation

An ordered arrangement of forces for a specific purpose and describes the general configuration of a unit on the ground.

*movement to contact

(Army) A type of offensive operation designed to develop the situation and to establish or regain contact.

mutual support

That support which units render each other against an enemy, because of their assigned tasks, their position relative to each other and to the enemy, and their inherent capabilities. (JP 3-31)

*objective

(Army) A location used to orient operations, phase operations, facilitate changes of direction, and provide for unity of effort.

*objective rally point

An easily identifiable point where all elements of the infiltrating unit assemble and prepare to attack the objective.

obscurant

Material that decreases the level of energy available for the functions of seekers, trackers, and vision enhancement devices. (ATP 3-11.50)

operational framework

A cognitive tool used to assist commanders and staffs in clearly visualizing and describing the application of combat power in time, space, purpose, and resources in the concept of operations. (ADP 1-01)

operation

A sequence of tactical actions with a common purpose and a unifying theme. (JP 1)

*operations in depth

The simultaneous application of combat power throughout an area of operations.

passage of lines

An operation in which a force moves forward or rearward through another force's combat positions with the intention of moving into or out of contact with the enemy. (JP 3-18)

*piecemeal commitment

The immediate employment of units in combat as they become available instead of waiting for larger aggregations of units to ensure mass, or the unsynchronized employment of available forces so that their combat power is not employed effectively.

*platoon

A subdivision of a company or troop consisting of two or more squads or sections.

*point of departure

The point where the unit crosses the line of departure and begins moving along a direction of attack.

position of relative advantage

A location or the establishment of a favorable condition within the area of operations that provides the commander with temporary freedom of action to enhance combat power over an enemy or influence the enemy to accept risk and move to a position of disadvantage. (ADP 3-0)

*primary position

The position that covers the enemy's most likely avenue of approach into the area of operations.

*probable line of deployment

A phase line that designates the location where the commander intends to deploy the unit into assault formation before beginning the assault.

protection warfighting function

The related tasks and systems that preserve the force so the commander can apply maximum combat power to accomplish the mission. (ADP 3-0)

*pursuit

A type of offensive operation designed to catch or cut off a hostile force attempting to escape, with the aim of destroying it.

rally point

An easily identifiable point on the ground at which units can reassemble and reorganize if they become dispersed. (ATP 3-21.20)

*rearward passage of lines

Occurs when a unit passes through another unit's positions while moving away from the enemy.

reconnaissance

A mission undertaken to obtain, by visual observation or other detection methods, information about the activities and resources of an enemy or adversary, or to secure data concerning the meteorological, hydrographic, or geographic characteristics of a particular area. (JP 2-0)

*reconnaissance in force

A type of reconnaissance operation designed to discover or test the enemy's strength, dispositions, and reactions or to obtain other information.

*reconnaissance objective

A terrain feature, geographic area, enemy force, adversary, or other mission or operational variable about which the commander wants to obtain additional information.

reconstitution

Those actions, including regeneration and reorganization, commanders plan and implement to restore units to a desired level of combat effectiveness commensurate with mission requirements and available resources. (JP 3-02)

relief in place

An operation in which, by direction of higher authority, all or part of a unit is replaced in an area by the incoming unit and the responsibilities of the replaced elements for the mission and the assigned zone of operations are transferred to the incoming unit. (JP 3-07.3)

*reserve

(Army) That portion of a body of troops that is withheld from action at the beginning of an engagement to be available for a decisive movement.

*retirement
> When a force out of contact moves away from the enemy.

*retrograde
> (Army) A type defensive operation that involves organized movement away from the enemy.

*route reconnaissance
> A type of reconnaissance operation to obtain detailed information of a specified route and all terrain from which the enemy could influence movement along that route.

rules of engagement
> Directives issued by competent military authority that delineate the circumstances and limitations under which United States forces will initiate and/or continue combat engagement with other forces encountered. (JP 3-84)

*science of tactics
> The understanding of those military aspects of tactics—capabilities, techniques, and procedures—that can be measured and codified.

*screen
> A type of security operation that primarily provides early warning to the protected force.

*section
> (Army) A tactical unit of the Army and Marine Corps smaller than a platoon and larger than a squad.

*security area
> That area occupied by a unit's security elements and includes the areas of influence of those security elements.

*security operations
> Those operations performed by commanders to provide early and accurate warning of enemy operations, to provide the forces being protected with time and maneuver space within which to react to the enemy, and to develop the situation to allow commanders to effectively use their protected forces.

*sequential relief in place
> Occurs when each element within the relieved unit is relieved in succession, from right to left or left to right, depending on how it is deployed.

*simultaneous relief in place
> Occurs when all elements are relieved at the same time.

situational understanding
> The product of applying analysis and judgment to relevant information to determine the relationships among the operational and mission variables. (ADP 6-0)

special reconnaissance
> Reconnaissance and surveillance actions conducted as a special operation in hostile, denied, or diplomatically and/or politically sensitive environments to collect or verify information of strategic or operational significance, employing military capabilities not normally found in conventional forces. (JP 3-05)

*squad
> A small military unit typically containing two or more fire teams.

*staggered relief in place
> Occurs when a commander relieves each element in a sequence determined by the tactical situation, not its geographical orientation.

Glossary

*striking force

A dedicated counterattack force in a mobile defense constituted with the bulk of available combat power.

*strong point

A heavily fortified battle position tied to a natural or reinforcing obstacle to create an anchor for the defense or to deny the enemy decisive or key terrain.

*subsequent position

A position that a unit expects to move to during the course of battle.

*supplementary position

A defensive position located within a unit's assigned area of operations that provides the best sectors of fire and defensive terrain along an avenue of approach that is not the primary avenue where the enemy is expected to attack.

*support by fire position

The general position from which a unit performs the tactical mission task of support by fire.

supporting distance

The distance between two units that can be traveled in time for one to come to the aid of the other and prevent its defeat by an enemy or ensure it regains control of a civil situation. (ADP 3-0)

supporting range

The distance one unit may be geographically separated from a second unit yet remain within the maximum range of the second unit's weapons systems. (ADP 3-0)

survivability

(Army) A quality or capability of military forces which permits them to avoid or withstand hostile actions or environmental conditions while retaining the ability to fulfill their primary mission. (ATP 3-37.34)

*survivability move

A move that involves rapidly displacing a unit, command post, or facility in response to direct and indirect fires, the approach of a threat or as a proactive measure based on intelligence, meteorological data, and risk assessment of enemy capabilities and intentions.

sustainment warfighting function

The related tasks and systems that provide support and services to ensure freedom of action, extend operational reach, and prolong endurance. (ADP 3-0)

tactical level of warfare

The level of warfare at which battles and engagements are planned and executed to achieve military objectives assigned to tactical units or task forces. (JP 3-0)

*tactical mobility

The ability of friendly forces to move and maneuver freely on the battlefield relative to the enemy.

*tactical road march

A rapid movement used to relocate units within an area of operations to prepare for combat operations.

*tactics

(Army) The employment, ordered arrangement, and directed actions of forces in relation to each other.

tempo

The relative speed and rhythm of military operations over time with respect to the enemy. (ADP 3-0)

*terrain management

The process of allocating terrain by establishing areas of operations, designating assembly areas, and specifying locations for units and activities to deconflict activities that might interfere with each other.

*time of attack

The moment the leading elements of the main body cross the line of departure, or in a limited-visibility attack, the point of departure.

*troop

A company-size unit in a cavalry organization.

*troop movement

The movement of Soldiers and units from one place to another by any available means.

*uncommitted force

A force that is not in contact with an enemy and is not already deployed on a specific mission or course of action.

warfighting function

A group of tasks and systems united by a common purpose that commanders use to accomplish missions and training objectives. (ADP 3-0)

*withdraw

To disengage from an enemy force and move in a direction away from the enemy.

*zone reconnaissance

A type of reconnaissance operation that involves a directed effort to obtain detailed information on all routes, obstacles, terrain, and enemy forces within a zone defined by boundaries.

References

All websites accessed on 15 July 2019.

REQUIRED PUBLICATIONS

These documents must be available to intended users of this publication:

DOD Dictionary of Military and Associated Terms. June 2019.

ADP 1-02. *Terms and Military Symbols*. 14 August 2018.

RELATED PUBLICATIONS

This publication references these publications.

JOINT PUBLICATIONS

Most joint publications are available online: https://www.jcs.mil/Doctrine/.

JP 1. *Doctrine for the Armed Forces of the United States*. 25 March 2013.

JP 2-0. *Joint Intelligence*. 22 October 2013.

JP 2-01. *Joint and National Intelligence Support to Military Operations*. 5 July 2017.

JP 3-0. *Joint Operations*. 17 January 2017.

JP 3-02. *Amphibious Operations*. 4 January 2019.

JP 3-03. *Joint Interdiction*. 9 September 2016.

JP 3-05. *Special Operations*. 16 July 2014.

JP 3-07.3. *Peace Operations*. 1 March 2018.

JP 3-08. *Interorganizational Cooperation*. 12 October 2016.

JP 3-09.3. *Close Air Support*. 10 June 2019.

JP 3-15. *Barriers, Obstacles, and Mine Warfare for Joint Operations*. 06 September 2016.

JP 3-18. *Joint Forcible Entry Operations*. 11 May 2017.

JP 3-31. *Joint Land Operations*. 24 February 2014.

JP 3-52. *Joint Airspace Control*. 13 November 2014.

JP 3-57. *Civil-Military Operations*. 9 July 2018.

JP 3-84. *Legal Support*. 02 August 2016.

JP 4-09. *Distribution Operations*. 14 March 2019.

ARMY PUBLICATIONS

Most Army doctrinal publications are available online: https://armypubs.army.mil/.

ADP 1-01. *Doctrine Primer*. 31 July 2019.

ADP 2-0. *Intelligence*. 31 July 2019.

ADP 3-0. *Operations*. 31 July 2019.

ADP 3-07. *Stability*. 31 July 2019.

ADP 3-28. *Defense Support of Civil Authorities*. 31 July 2019.

ADP 3-37. *Protection*. 31 July 2019.

ADP 4-0. *Sustainment*. 31 July 2019.

ADP 5-0. *The Operations Process.* 31 July 2019.
ADP 6-0. *Mission Command: Command and Control of Army Forces.* 31 July 2019.
ATP 2-01.3. *Intelligence Preparation of the Battlefield.* 1 March 2019.
ATP 3-07.5. *Stability Techniques.* 31 August 2012.
ATP 3-11.32/MCWP 10-10E.8/NTTP 3-11.37/AFTTP 3-2.46. *Multi-Service Tactics, Techniques, and Procedures for Chemical, Biological, Radiological, and Nuclear Passive Defense.* 13 May 2016.
ATP 3-11.36/MCRP 10-10E.1/NTTP 3-11.34/AFTTP 3-2.70. *Multi-Service Tactics, Techniques, and Procedures for Chemical, Biological, Radiological, and Nuclear Planning.* 24 September 2018.
ATP 3-11.50. *Battlefield Obscuration.* 15 May 2014.
ATP 3-21.20. *Infantry Battalion.* 28 December 2017.
ATP 3-34.5/MCRP 4-11B. *Environmental Considerations.* 10 August 2015.
ATP 3-34.80. *Geospatial Engineering.* 22 February 2017.
ATP 3-37.10/MCRP 3-40D.13. *Base Camps.* 27 January 2017.
ATP 3-37.34/MCTP 3-34C. *Survivability Operations.* 16 April 2018.
ATP 3-90.4/MCWP 3-17.8. *Combined Arms Mobility.* 8 March 2016.
ATP 3-90.8/MCWP 3-17.5. *Combined Arms Countermobility Operations.* 17 September 2014.
ATP 3-90.40. *Combined Arms Countering Weapons of Mass Destruction.* 29 June 2017.
ATP 3-91. *Division Operations.* 17 October 2014.
ATP 3-91.1/AFTTP 3-2.86. *The Joint Air Ground Integration Center.* 17 April 2019.
ATP 3-92. *Corps Operations.* 7 April 2016.
ATP 4-01.45/MCRP 3-40F.7/AFTTP 3-2.58. *Multi-Service Tactics, Techniques, and Procedures for Tactical Convoy Operations.* 22 February 2017.
ATP 4-16. *Movement Control.* 5 April 2013.
FM 1-04. *Legal Support to the Operational Army.* 18 March 2013.
FM 2-0. *Intelligence.* 6 July 2018.
FM 3-0. *Operations.* 6 October 2017.
FM 3-01. *U.S. Army Air and Missile Defense Operations.* 2 November 2015.
FM 3-04. *Army Aviation.* 29 July 2015.
FM 3-09. *Field Artillery Operations and Fire Support.* 4 April 2014.
FM 3-13. *Information Operations.* 6 December 2016.
FM 3-16. *The Army in Multinational Operations.* 8 April 2014.
FM 3-50. *Army Personnel Recovery.* 2 September 2014.
FM 3-52. *Airspace Control.* 20 October 2016.
FM 3-63. *Detainee Operations.* 28 April 2014.
FM 3-90-1. *Offense and Defense Volume 1.* 22 March 2013.
FM 3-90-2. *Reconnaissance, Security, and Tactical Enabling Tasks Volume 2.* 22 March 2013.
FM 3-94. *Theater Army, Corps, and Division Operations.* 21 April 2014.
FM 3-96. *Brigade Combat Team.* 8 October 2015.
FM 3-98. *Reconnaissance and Security Operations.* 1 July 2015.
FM 4-01. *Army Transportation Operations.* 3 April 2014.
FM 4-95. *Logistics Operations.* 1 April 2014.
FM 6-0. *Commander and Staff Organization and Operations.* 5 May 2014.
FM 6-02. *Signal Support to Operations.* 22 January 2014.

FM 27-10. *The Law of Land Warfare*. 18 July 1956.

OBSOLETE PUBLICATION

Field Service Regulations United States Army. 2 November 1923.
http://cgsc.contentdm.oclc.org/cdm/compoundobject/collection/p4013coll9/id/126/rec/2.

PRESCRIBED FORMS

This section contains no entries.

REFERENCED FORMS

Unless otherwise indicated, DA forms are available on the Army Publishing Directorate Web site: https://armypubs.army.mil/.

DA Form 2028. *Recommended Changes to Publications and Blank Forms*.

This page intentionally left blank.

Index

Entries are by paragraph number.

A

audacity, 3-4
avenue of approach, defined, 2-46
aviation forces, 4-60
axis of advance, defined, 3-24

B

basic load, defined, 3-101
basic tactical concepts, 2-12–2-79
battalion, defined, 2-92
battalion task force, defined, 2-94
battalions and squadrons, 2-92–2-95
batteries, 2-90, 2-94
battery, defined, 2-90
battle, defined, 1-5
battle handover line, defined, 3-25
battle position, defined, 4-22
battle positions, 4-22–4-26
breakout, defined, 4-111
breakout, 4-111
brigade, airspace management, 2-40–2-42
brigade combat team, defined, 2-97
brigades, regiments, and groups, 2-96–2-99
bypass criteria, defined, 3-24

C

characteristics, of the defense, 4-5–4-14
of the offense, 3-3–3-12
chemical, biological, radiological, and nuclear defense, 4-103–4-106
choices and tradeoffs, 1-36–1-49
civil-military operations, defined, 2-25
clearance of fires, 2-27–2-30
defined, 2-27
close combat, defined, 3-57
combat, effects on Soldiers, 1-17–1-20
combat information, 1-37
combat power, defined, 1-26
mass the effects of, 4-56–4-60
combined arms, defined, 1-21, 2-47
committed force, defined, 2-48
common, defensive planning considerations, 4-37–4-115
offensive control measures, 3-19–3-38
offensive planning considerations, 3-39–3-125
tactical concepts and echelons, 2-1–2-107
communications, degraded, 3-53–3-55
companies, 2-90–2-91
company, defined, 2-90
company team, defined, 2-91
concentration, 3-5–3-6 4-9–4-11
concept of operations, defined, 2-49
concepts, basic tactical, 2-12–2-79
concepts and echelons, common tactical, 2-1–2-107
conditions of uncertainty, decision making under, 1-15–1-16
conduct, population and resource control, 4-110
considerations, environmental, 2-45
consolidate gains, defined, 1-31
control measures, common defensive, 4-21–4-36
common offensive, 3-19–3-38
direct fire, 4-27
target, 3-37
coordinating altitude, defined, 2-38
coordination measures, fire support, 4-30
corps, 2-104–2-106
airspace management, 2-36–2-39
countermobility, 3-75–3-79, 4-64–4-67
cover, defined, 5-7
creative and flexible, application of means, 1-13–1-14
crew, defined, 2-86

D

decision making, under conditions of uncertainty, 1-15–1-16
decisive engagement, defined, 2-50
decisive operation, defined, 2-79
decisive terrain, defined, 3-58
defeat in detail, defined, 2-51
defeat mechanism, defined, 2-11
defense, 4-1–4-127
air and missile, 3-97–3-199, 4-82–4-84
characteristics of, 4-5–4-14
chemical, biological, radiological, and nuclear, 4-103–4-106
missile, 3-97–3-99
purposes of, 4-1–4-4
transition to, 3-118–3-122
defensive control measures, common, 4-21–4-36
defensive planning considerations, common, 4-37–4-127

Index

Entries are by paragraph number.

degraded communications, 3-53–3-55
delay, defined, 4-20
deliberate operation, defined, 1-34
deliberate, versus hasty operations, 1-33–1-49
detachment, defined, 2-90
detachments, 2-90–2-91
direct fire control measures, 4-27
direction of attack, defined, 3-26
disengagement line, 4-28
dismounted infantry forces, 3-60, 4-58–4-59
disrupt the enemy attack, 4-55
disruption, 4-6
division, airspace management, 2-36–2-39
 defined, 2-100
divisions, 2-100–2-103

E

echelons, 2-83–2-84
echelons and concepts, common tactical, 2-1–2-107
economy of force, defined, 2-52
effects of combat on Soldiers, 1-17–1-20
encirclement operations, 2-53
enemy airborne and air assault attacks, 4-68–4-69
enemy attack, disrupt, 4-55
engagement, defined, 1-4
engagement area, 4-29
 defined, 2-54
ensure mutual support, 4-61
environmental considerations, 2-45
exfiltration, 4-112
exploit the advantages of terrain, 4-51–4-54
exploitation, defined, 3-17

F

field armies, 2-107
final coordination line, defined, 3-27
final protective fire, defined, 4-30

fire support coordination measure, defined, 2-29
fire support coordination measures, 4-30
fire team, defined, 2-85
fires, 3-87–3-99 4-77–4-184
fires warfighting function, defined, 2-10
fixing force, defined, 4-17
flank, defined, 2-55
flanking position, defined, 2-58
flanks, 2-55–2-58
flexibility, 4-7
forces, armored, 3-59, 4-57
 aviation, 3-61–3-63, 4-60
 dismounted infantry, 3-60, 4-58–4-59
 Stryker, 3-59, 4-57
forms of maneuver, defined, 2-81
forms of the defense, 2-82
forward edge of the battle area, defined, 4-31
forward line of own troops, defined, 3-32
forward passage of lines, defined, 5-18
framework, operational, 2-69–2-70
fundamentals, tactical, 1-1–1-49

G

groups, 2-99
guard, defined, 5-07

H

hasty operation, defined, 1-33
hasty versus deliberate operations, 1-33–1-35
health service support, 3-108

I

indirect fires, Army in the defense, 4-78–4-81
infantry forces, dismounted, 3-60, 4-58–4-59
information collection, 2-21–2-24
intelligence, 3-83–3-86, 4-73–4-76
intelligence operations, defined, 2-21

intelligence warfighting function, defined, 2-10

J

joint fires, in the defense, 4-78–4-81
 in the offense, 3-88–3-96
joint interdependence, 2-1
joint operations, principles of, 2-2

K

key terrain, defined, 3-57

L

level of warfare, tactical, 1-3–1-7
limit of advance, defined, 3-29
line of contact, defined, 3-30
line of departure, defined, 3-31
linkup, defined, 4-115
local security, defined, 2-60
logistics, 3-101–3-107

M

main battle area, 4-33–4-34
 defined, 4-33
main body, defined, 1-48
main effort, weighting, 2-79
maneuver, 3-56–3-58, 4-8, 4-50–4-72
 defined, 2-61
mass and concentration, 4-9–4-11
mass the effects of combat power, 4-56–4-60
methods of troop movement, 5-12
minimum-essential stability tasks, 2-43–2-44
missile defense, 3-97–3-99, 4-82–4-84
command and control, 3-42–3-55
 in the defense, 4-42–4-49
command and control warfighting function, defined, 2-10
mission variables, 2-4–2-5
mobile defense, defined, 4-17
mobility, 3-70–3-74, 4-62–4-63
 assured, 3-68–3-69
mobility tasks, 4-73
 defined, 3-70

Index

Entries are by paragraph number.

movement and maneuver, 3-56–3-67, 4-50–4-72
movement and maneuver warfighting function, defined, 2-10
movement control, 5-13
  defined, 2-26
movement formation, defined, 3-64
movement formations, 3-64–3-66
movement techniques, 3-65
movement to contact, defined, 3-14
mutual support, 2-65–2-67
  defined, 2-65
  ensure, 4-61

N-O

objective, defined, 3-32
objective rally point, defined, 3-35
obscurant, defined, 3-82
obscuration, 3-80–3-82 4-70–4-72
offense, 3-1–3-125
  characteristics, 3-3–3-12
  purposes, 3-1–3-2
  transition to, 4-120–4-126
offensive operations, types, 3-13–3-18
operation, defined, 2-68
operational framework, 2-69–2-70
  defined, 2-69
operational variables, 2-3
operations, hasty versus deliberate, 1-33–1-35
  survivability, 3-79, 4-96–4-102
operations in depth, defined, 4-12
operations process, 3-43–3-51

P

passage of lines, 5-18–5-20
  defined, 5-18
personnel recovery, 2-32
physical security and antiterrorism, 4-107–4-109
piecemeal commitment, defined, 2-71
planning considerations, common defensive, 4-37–4-127

common offensive, 3-39–3-125
platoon, defined, 2-89
point of departure, defined, 3-33
population and resource control, conduct, 4-110
position of relative advantage, defined, 2-61
preparation, 4-13
primary position, defined, 4-25
principles of joint operations, 2-2
probable line of deployment, defined, 3-34
problems, solving tactical, 1-23–1-32
protection, 3-109–3-114, 4-92–4-95
protection warfighting function, defined, 2-10
purposes, of the defense, 4-1–4-4
  of the offense, 3-1–3-2
pursuit, defined, 3-18

R

rally point, defined, 3-35
rearward passage of lines, defined, 5-18
reconnaissance, 5-1–5-15
  defined, 5-1
reconnaissance in force, defined, 5-5
reconnaissance objective, defined, 5-2
reconstitution, defined, 2-72
regiments, 2-98
relief in place, 5-14–5-17
  defined, 5-14
reserve, defined, 2-73
resource control, conduct, 4-110
retirement, defined, 4-20
retrograde, 4-19–4-20
  defined, 4-19
  transition to, 4-116–4-119
risk, 1-36–1-49
rotary-wing aviation, 3-61–3-63
route reconnaissance, defined, 5-5
rules of engagement, defined, 2-74

S

science of tactics, 1-21–1-22
  defined, 1-21
screen, defined, 5-7
section, defined, 2-88
security, 2-31 4-14
security area, defined, 1-46
security operations, 5-6–5-10
security tasks, defined, 2-24
situational understanding, defined, 1-15
Soldiers' load, 3-67
solving tactical problems, 1-23–1-32
special reconnaissance, defined, 5-5
squad, defined, 2-87
squadrons, 2-92
stability tasks, minimum essential, 2-43–2-44
striking force, defined, 4-17
strong point, defined, 4-25
Stryker forces, 3-59, 4-57
subsequent position, defined, 4-25
supplementary position, defined, 4-25
support by fire position, defined, 3-36
supporting distance, defined, 2-75
supporting range, defined, 2-76
surprise, 3-7–3-9
survivability, defined, 3-79
survivability move, defined, 4-54
survivability operations, 4-96–4-102
sustainment, 3-100–3-108, 4-85–4-91
sustainment warfighting function, defined, 2-10

T

tactical, concepts, basic, 2-12–2-79
  doctrinal taxonomy, 2-6–2-9
  enabling operations, 5-1–5-20
  level of warfare, 1-3–1-7
  solving problems, 1-23–1-32

Entries are by paragraph number.

tactical level of warfare, defined, 1-3
tactical mobility, defined, 2-77
tactical road march, defined, 5-11
tactics, 1-1–1-2
    art of, 1-9–1-12
    defined, 1-1
    science of, 1-21–1-22
target, 3-36
target control measures, 3-37
taxonomy, tactical doctrinal, 2-6–2-9
team development between commanders, 3-52
tempo, 3-10–3-12
    defined, 3-10
terrain, exploit the advantages of, 4-51–4-54
terrain management, defined, 2-19
time of attack, defined, 3-38
tradeoff and choices, 1-36–1-41
transition, 3-115–3-125, 4-116–4-127
    to the defense, 3-118–3-122
    to the offense, 4-120–4-126
    to the retrograde, 4-116
    to stability operations, 3-123–3-125, 4-127
troop, defined, 2-90
troop movement, 5-11–5-13
    defined, 5-11
    methods of, 5-12
troops, 2-90–2-91

U

uncommitted force, defined, 2-78
unmanned aircraft systems, 3-63

V

variables, mission, 2-4–2-5
    operational, 2-3

W

warfighting function, defined, 2-10
weighting the decisive operation or main effort, 2-79
withdraw, defined, 4-20

X-Y-Z

zone reconnaissance, defined, 5-5

Made in the USA
Columbia, SC
29 July 2024

39580377R00059